# TECHNOLOGY STRATEGIES
# FOR MUSIC EDUCATION

Second Edition

**Authors**

Thomas E. Rudolph
Floyd Richmond
David Mash
Peter Webster
William I. Bauer
Kim Walls

---

**Editor**

Floyd Richmond

**Editorial
Consultant**

Scott Watson

## TI:ME
The Technology Institute for Music Educators

**Contributors**
**Authors:**

    Thomas E. Rudolph, TI:ME President, Haverford School District

    Floyd Richmond, Valley Forge Christian College

    David Mash, Berklee College of Music

    Peter Webster, Northwestern University

    William I. Bauer, Case Western Reserve University

    Kim Walls, Auburn University

**Editors:**

    John Dunphy, Villanova University, 1998 Editor

    George Pinchock, Villanova University, 1998 Editor

    Steven Estrella, Shearspire Corp, 2002 Editor

    Peter McAllister, Ball State University, 2002 Editor

    Floyd Richmond, Valley Forge Christian College, 2005 Editor

    Scott Watson, Parkland School District, 2005 Editorial Consultant

**Cover design:** Judy Bolinger Bucci

**TI:ME Logo design:** Steven Estrella, Shearspire, Inc.

Copyright © 2005 Technology Institute for Music Educators
305 Maple Avenue
Wyncote, PA 19095
timemused@ti-me.org
http://www.ti-me.org

ISBN 0-634-09060-7

Printed in the United States of America

Visit Hal Leonard online at http://www.halleonard.com

# Table of Contents

INTRODUCTION ........................................................................................................ v
      The Technology Institute for Music Educators (TI:ME)
      Purpose of This Publication


SECTION 1: TECHNOLOGY IN MUSIC EDUCATION: AN OVERVIEW ........ 1
      Technology in Society
      Students and Technology
      Technology as a Tool
      Active Learning


SECTION 2: AREAS OF COMPETENCY IN MUSIC TECHNOLOGY ............... 3
      Electronic Musical Instruments
      Music Production
      Music Notation Software
      Technology-Assisted Learning
      Multimedia
      Productivity Tools, Classroom and Lab Management


SECTION 3: THE NATIONAL STANDARDS FOR ARTS EDUCATION ......... 15
      Background
      Categories of Learning
      The Nine National Standards
      The Achievement Standards
      The Technology Areas of Competency and the National Standards
      Opportunity-to-Learn Standards for Music Technology


SECTION 4: STANDARDS OF THE INTERNATIONAL SOCIETY
      FOR TECHNOLOGY IN EDUCATION .................................................... 23
      Introduction
      NETS-S
      NETS-T
      NETS-A
      TI:ME Strategies and the ISTE Standards
      Conclusion

SECTION 5:  STUDENT AND TEACHER STRATEGIES AND ACTIVITIES ... 31

    Content Standard #1:      Singing, alone and with others, a varied repertoire of music

    Content Standard #2:      Performing on instruments, alone and with others,
                        a varied repertoire of music

    Content Standard #3:      Improvising melodies, variations, and accompaniments

    Content Standard #4:      Composing and arranging music within specified guidelines

    Content Standard #5:      Reading and notating music

    Content Standard #6:      Listening to, analyzing and describing music

    Content Standard #7:      Evaluating music and music performances

    Content Standard #8:      Understanding relationships between music, the other arts,
                        and disciplines outside the arts

    Content Standard #9:      Understanding music in relation to history and culture

SECTION 6:  INFORMATION PROCESSING, COMPUTER SYSTEMS,
            AND LAB MANAGEMENT ...................................................... 49

    Information Processing

    Computer Systems

    Lab Management

SECTION 7:  ASSESSMENT AND MUSIC TECHNOLOGY ............................. 61

    Designing Assessments

    Assessment Instruments

    Technology-based Assessment Tools

    Summary

SECTION 8:  CREATIVE THINKING AND MUSIC TECHNOLOGY ............... 69

    Introduction

    Teaching Creatively

    Encouraging Creative Thinking in Students

Appendix A:
    Technology Strategies Organized by MENC Content Standards ................. 79

Appendix B:
    Technology Strategies Organized by TI:ME Technology Areas ................... 93

Appendix C:
    Technology Strategies Related to Information Processing,
    Computer Systems, and Lab Management ................................................109

Appendix D:
    Strategies and Standards at a Glance ........................................................111

Appendix E:
    Web Resources ........................................................................................113

# INTRODUCTION

**Technology Institute for Music Educators (TI:ME)**

TI:ME is a non-profit organization whose goals and objectives include the development of in-service teacher training and certification in the area of music technology. It is devoted to helping music teachers learn how to integrate the tools of technology into the music curriculum. It supports the National Standards for Arts Education as adopted by the Music Educators National Conference (MENC) as well as the National Educational Technology Standards (NETS) of the International Society for Technology in Education (ISTE).

**Purpose of This Publication**

The Technology Strategies for Music Education are designed for in-service K-12 music teachers. This document contains strategies for integrating technology into the music curriculum, and the areas of competency leading to TI:ME certification.

This publication is meant to be an overview. It is not a course of study, it is not meant to be a textbook, and it does not represent a full description of the curriculum or courses endorsed by TI:ME.

**A Word About The Second Edition**

The second edition of this textbook addresses the developments in music technology software and hardware since 1998 when the first edition of this book was released. The numerous advances in computer software and hardware in the years since 1998 make a second edition necessary. For example, in past years there has been a trend by music software publishers away from creating stand-alone MIDI sequencers. As these programs matured, they increasingly integrated digital audio. Since the original Technology Strategies had a category entitled sequencing, it was necessary to update both the category and terminology to more closely match today's practices. The former category entitled sequencing has been renamed music production. Another change is the increased facility of individuals getting onto and navigating the Internet. In 1997 and 1998, the Internet was relatively new. Today, the Internet is available virtually everywhere. Much of the emphasis that was required in past years can be assumed as common knowledge today. The Internet has also matured substantially. For instance, it was common for a web page in the mid to late 1990's to consist primarily of a pictures, words, and links. Today's browsers support a host of additional features including interactive audio, video and instruction. These developments create overlap between the Internet and other categories such as instructional software, music production and multimedia production. The authors have decided that those parts of the Internet which can be addressed in others areas should be and that there is now little need to instruct teachers on the remaining content: how to use the Internet. The Internet category in the original technology strategies has been folded into the others. A detailed explanation of the revised TI:ME categories is found in Sections 1 and 2.

Finally, a second edition allows additional content to be included. The authors have increased the number of strategies for integrating music technology into music instruction by one third. Additional content also includes new chapters on standards, assessment and creativity. These new chapters address areas of importance to all music teachers, but especially those who are using music technology.

Because of the rapid pace of development in music technology, there will always be ongoing changes. The authors are confident that the future holds new and, as of yet, unimagined applications. TI:ME will continue to monitor the trends and work to inform music educators of the impact on the classroom.

# SECTION 1:
# TECHNOLOGY IN MUSIC EDUCATION:
# AN OVERVIEW

David Mash, Berklee College of Music

## Technology in Society

The use of technology is pervasive in modern society. From digital wristwatches and cellular telephones, to fax machines, electronic mail, and instant messaging, the use of technology has become ubiquitous. It is difficult to imagine business being conducted today without these technology tools. Technology has also impacted every form of entertainment—exciting digital effects pervade modern movies; animated features are completely computer-generated; sports broadcasts are digitally enhanced to allow viewers to better experience the excitement of the game; home video games provide thrilling three-dimensional worlds, with virtual environments only dreamed of a few years ago; and live concerts are augmented by sound and video reinforcements. Digital audio on compact discs has completely replaced analog recordings on vinyl or magnetic tape. And online music in mp3 and other digital file formats are challenging CDs as the primary means of digital music distribution. Online music stores linked to portable music players via computers continue to change how we obtain and listen to music. It is not possible to turn back—technology is here to stay.

## Students and Technology

Students are growing up in a different environment than that of their teachers. Young children have never known a time without the existence of cell phones, computers, digital music, MIDI, video games, or instant messaging. Yet many of their teachers may clearly remember times in their own lives when these technologies were not available. Teachers must prepare students for their future and this includes the technologies they will use.

Music teachers have long used technology in their teaching. Overhead projectors, pianos, and music playback devices (records or tape) are mainstays of classroom teachers. These have become easy-to-use tools and are taken for granted, but they, too, were once state-of-the-art, emergent technologies. Like these tools, today's technologies can support teaching activities and improve students' abilities to learn.

## Technology as a Tool

Current technology tools can help teachers be more effective, both in and outside the classroom. Sound and notation can be integrated in ways never before possible. With some software programs, the recording plays while the score scrolls automatically in time with the music. Alter a note in the score and immediately hear the change. Musical excerpts can be played with the single click of a button, then replayed with no rewind time, or searching for a starting point. Click the button and the phrase will play from precise start to end with fraction-of-a-second accuracy. Virtual orchestras allow us to experiment with tempo changes, transpositions, new instrumentations, and changes in modality and instantly hear the results.

New looping software allows students to create music from pre-recorded building blocks, mixing musical styles and instrumentation to create new musical compositions. This allows untrained general music students to actively create music much the way young art students use crayons and paper to make visual art. With these new tools we can better support musical creativity and inspire more students to become actively engaged in the music making process.

## Active Learning

Most importantly, today's new technologies hold the key to improved music learning. Placing the tools of technology into students' hands guides them to active music making. General music classes no longer need to be passive listening experiences. Technology allows students to become actively involved in the study of music while having the satisfaction of creating something themselves. Research indicates that when students become active participants in learning they gain confidence, learn more effectively, and are motivated to study further. Technology can help attract students into the music curriculum. It will help develop critical thinking and problem solving skills. Students will learn to appreciate music as an art, and become participants in the joy of music-making.

# SECTION 2:
# AREAS OF COMPETENCY
# IN MUSIC TECHNOLOGY

David Mash, Berklee College of Music

The *Technology Institute for Music Educators* was formed in 1994, and originally identified seven areas of music technology that were directly applicable to music instruction in support of the National Standards for Arts Education. Since that time, technology has continued to develop, and its use in education has matured. Some applications have converged to the point that in 2004, the board of directors for the Technology Institute for Music Educators decided to revisit the areas of competency to determine if the original seven categories were still valid. The result of this review has led the organization to revise these areas of competency into six categories:

1. Electronic Musical Instruments
   a. Keyboards
   b. Controllers (Other)
   c. Synthesizers and Samplers
   d. Ensemble Performance
2. Music Production
   a. Data Types
       i. MIDI
       ii. Digital Audio
   b. Processes
       i. Sequencing
       ii. Looping
       iii. Signal Processing
       iv. Sound Design
3. Music Notation Software
4. Technology-Assisted Learning
   a. Instructional Software
   b. Accompaniment/Practice Tools
   c. Internet-based Learning

5. Multimedia
   a. Multimedia Authoring
      i. Web Pages
      ii. Presentations (PowerPoint, Keynote)
      iii. Movie/DVD
   b. Digital Image Capturing (Scanning, Still/Video Camera)
   c. Internet
   d. Electronic Portfolios
6. Productivity Tools, Classroom and Lab Management
   a. Productivity Tools (Text Editor, Spreadsheet, Database, etc.)
   b. Computer Systems (CPU, I/O Devices, Storage Devices/Media, etc.)
   c. Lab Management Systems (Group Practice Systems)
   d. Networks (Network Manager Software, Server, etc.)

The section below presents these six areas of competency in greater detail, and explains the importance of each.

## Electronic Musical Instruments

Electronic musical instruments may be defined as those that generate their sound electronically, rather than acoustically. Two examples are synthesizers and digital pianos. Electronic instruments generally have two components, a controller (keyboard, strings, fretboard, percussion pads) and a sound generator; these two components may be separate units or contained in one package as is the case with a digital piano.

With acoustic instruments, the generation of sound is linked to the control of that sound. For example, a piano makes a sound when a key is played with force, a violin produces a sound when the bow is drawn across a string. The physical action is directly linked to the sound production. This is not always true with electronic musical instruments. Instrumental controllers, like electronic wind instruments, may make absolutely no sound by themselves. Instead, they produce a control signal that is transmitted to a sound-generating device by way of MIDI—the Musical Instrument Digital Interface. MIDI allows this separation of electronic instruments into controller and sound generator, which opens a new world of sound possibilities for the performer.

Michael Brecker, one of the great saxophone players of our time, also plays an electronic wind instrument. It allows him to use his playing technique to control sounds other than those available through the saxophone alone. He can play notes over a seven-octave range at dynamic levels from pianissimo to fortissimo and with timbres ranging from a violin to a gunshot. In addition to this broad sonic palette, the wind controller allows him to store his performance in a computer's memory. He can then play, store, edit, and print his performance in standard music notation. MIDI has changed the world of professional music making. Electronic musical instruments may also be used to support music education by playing prerecorded MIDI performances as accompaniment, and as an aid in teaching basic arranging techniques and sound design.

Music teachers need to know how MIDI connections are made between instruments and/or computers and how to use MIDI in the classroom. They need to understand how to create layered and split keyboard sounds for performances. They also need to be able to choose and edit sounds from stored libraries and create sounds using an electronic instrument. Understanding how synthesizers and digital samplers work supports these processes, both in and outside the music classroom.

Students can use electronic instruments as musical crayons, creating simple to complex musical pieces while gaining dexterity and technique. They can learn musical processes with electronic keyboards and have fun at the same time. Research has shown that active participation in keyboard studies produce increased student performance on math and science problems that involve spatial-temporal reasoning.[1]

Music teachers can integrate electronic instruments into existing ensembles, or can create entirely new electronic ensembles. Teachers need to know how to blend electronic sounds with acoustic instruments, how to operate sound reinforcement equipment, and how to set up and connect a variety of electronic instruments and devices to present effective ensemble concerts in the school environment.

**Music Production**

Technology has forever changed the way music is produced, recorded, and distributed. An understanding of new music production techniques is essential for today's music teacher. Incorporating music production technologies into the music classroom can help expose students to contemporary music making practice, engage students in this process, and instill confidence in their abilities to be musically creative and productive.

Music teachers need to understand the types of data involved in producing music

---

[1] Rauscher, Frances H. "Music Exposure and the Development of Spatial Intelligence in Children." Bulletin of the Council for Research in Music Education. n142, p35-47, Fall 1999.

with technology, as well as the various processes and procedures used today. MIDI data is control information, which describes musical performance. What notes are played, how loud they will sound, and a variety of phrasing techniques are sent as control information within the MIDI data stream. MIDI control information can also be used to set the levels of different instrumental parts in a project, thereby automating the final mixing process in a musical production.

Acoustic and electric sounds may be stored as digitized audio and used within music production software. Music teachers need to know how to record, store, and manipulate digital audio data. Furthermore, understanding the different applications of audio and MIDI data within the music production process has become increasingly important, as software synthesizers create digital audio under MIDI control, blurring the differentiation between these data types.

Today's music teacher also needs to be familiar, if not proficient, with the various processes for working with audio and MIDI data. Teachers should help students understand the music of their time, the processes involved in creating that music, and how to actively apply technology tools in the music production process. Contemporary music production techniques include sequencing, looping, signal processing, and sound design.

A musical performance consists of a series of sounds played in time with appropriate tempo and dynamic changes. MIDI data, however, consists of a stream of information or note events generated by the electronic controller device (keyboard, guitar, wind, percussion, etc.). As the musician performs, MIDI transmits which notes were played, their dynamic levels, and when the notes were stopped. This information can be stored in the order (sequence) played allowing the MIDI performance to be played back at a later time. A device or computer program that stores and retrieves this information is called a MIDI sequencer. When the sequencer plays the MIDI data, the sound generator produces the sound just as if the musician was again performing the music.

Today's MIDI sequencers are capable of storing large amounts of data. They are often designed to emulate a multi-track tape recorder, a familiar metaphor for most musicians. A musician may record different musical parts onto separate tracks of the MIDI sequencer. Each track of the sequence may be assigned to a different instrumental timbre, allowing a single musician to create complex performances of complete compositions. Unlike the tape recorder, the MIDI sequencer provides the musician with powerful and intuitive editing tools, which permit changes and corrections without rerecording. Once stored, the music can be edited in its entirety, by individual tracks, by groups of notes within a track, or by individual notes. Tempo can be changed without altering the pitch. Transposition can be accomplished with a few simple commands. The music can be viewed in standard notation, as a list of events, or in graphic piano roll form. The MIDI sequencing file can then be stored as a Standard MIDI File (SMF) for transfer to other MIDI software programs or hardware devices.

Teachers should be able to enter notes in a MIDI sequence either one at time (step-time) or by performing (real-time). They should know how to enter musical expressions by changing controller values to produce a more musical performance. At advanced levels, teachers should know how to produce transcriptions in standard music notation, use advanced editing and production techniques, perform complex mixing processes, and integrate digital audio with MIDI data in the sequencer environment.

MIDI sequencers are not only valuable for music production—they are valuable educational tools. Teachers can generate accompaniments for their choirs, classes, or instrumental groups, either by creating original sequences or by using commercially available Standard MIDI Files. Teachers can demonstrate orchestration and arranging techniques allowing students to immediately hear the example. Tempo, transposition, timbre, and dynamics also can be easily controlled and changed.

Students can use a MIDI sequencer to apply musical concepts learned in class to prerecorded sequences. They can learn how dynamics, tempo change, orchestration, and transposition produce musical nuance and expression. Students can practice performance on traditional acoustic instruments using the MIDI sequencer as accompaniment to ensure they are playing in time, in tune, and learning the piece in context. Combined with an electronic instrument, the MIDI sequencer can become a musical tool allowing students to gain confidence in expressing themselves through music.

The process of creating music by superimposing repeating snippets of digital audio or MIDI data is known as "looping." Special looping software tools allow short segments of music to be combined together in a musical fashion, without limitation of key, tempo, or musical style. Fast computer processing allows for tempos and keys of different recordings to be automatically matched, allowing music from very differing styles to be combined in new and exciting ways. Loops from musical styles and cultures that might seem extremely remote and unrelated can be juxtaposed to create new styles and new mix musics from around the world.

Today's music teacher needs to understand how these software tools operate, how to access music data in loop form, how these loops are imported into the production process, how to guide students in the crafting of musical phrases using loops, and how to put all of this into the larger context of music production processes. Teachers also have the opportunity to expose students to music of different cultures, and help them understand the building blocks of musical style and form through the use of looping tools.

As computers have become faster and more powerful, software now allows us to digitally process audio in real time. Digital Signal Processing (DSP) can be used within the music production process in many ways, from simply enhancing sound through techniques such as adding reverb, echo, or equalization to completely transforming audio, rendering it literally unrecognizable from its original sound.

Music teachers need to more fully understand sound, and how various signal processing techniques can be used to enhance audio in the production process. Teachers need to know how to effectively add effects such as reverb, chorus, and echo; how to improve clarity of a mix using equalization; and how to employ these concepts within standard production tools. These skills will not only come in handy when supervising students in their production projects, but can be useful in live performance and for improving the sound quality in recordings of student performances.

Synthesizers, either hardware or software, provide powerful controls over sound generation. Understanding how these controls affect sound, and how to use them creatively is the essence of sound design. Music teachers need to understand the basic techniques used in synthesizers to generate sound, and how to manipulate the controls to change these sounds. Teaching students about the fundamental building blocks of musical sound—pitch, timbre, and loudness can help them better appreciate music, and make cross-curricular connections to math and science. The ability to make meaningful changes in an instrument's sound can help engage students in critical listening, as well as foster creative music production.

**Music Notation Software**

Music notation software is designed to produce and print scores, extract and transpose individual parts, and generate MIDI performances. Once the data is entered, pieces can be transposed and parts can be prepared for a variety of instrumentations. Because music notation software can also output MIDI data, scores can be played through a MIDI instrument. Changes made to the notation are instantly heard upon playback. By using an ink-jet or laser printer, teachers can print out easy to read, professional-looking scores and parts.

Most notation software programs provide basic page layout capabilities, display of lyrics and chord symbols, and various graphic tools for non-standard notation techniques. Some notation programs also allow the data to be viewed and edited as MIDI information, allowing control over performance expression.

Teachers should be able to enter and layout a complete score, create parts, and integrate notation files into word processing software for text handouts and exams. They should also be able to integrate notation software into their teaching, demonstrating relationships between symbol and sound and guide students in the use of this software as a creative tool for composition.

Students can use music notation programs to learn the basics of notation and to hear what they write. Notes may be entered in a variety of ways including step-entry and real-time performance. Once entered, the notes may be edited, transposed, cut, copied, pasted, and expression markings added.

**Technology-Assisted Learning**

There are many software applications available to support music education. Those specifically designed to assist instruction are often called Computer-Assisted Instructional software, or CAI for short. Commercially available CAI software programs are designed to help students learn music theory and music history, to develop ear-training or instrumental skills, and to drill and test knowledge in a variety of areas.

Teachers should have a broad familiarity with available instructional software. They should understand how to install, use, and integrate these programs into their music curriculum taking full advantage of the record-keeping, evaluation, and instructional support CAI software provides. Instructional software can provide students with a patient practice partner, allowing self-paced progress through subject matter. Class work and progress can also be recorded using CAI software.

Powerful software is also available to support the development of instrumental technique and performance skills. These applications are generally grouped as intelligent accompaniment and practice tools. Students can access large libraries of pre-recorded accompaniments and practice with excellent backing tracks. Unlike pre-recorded audio, these accompaniments can be transposed, played at any tempo, and altered to play back in differing styles. Intelligent accompaniment software will "listen" to the student's performance and track pitch and timing accuracy, giving students meaningful support in playing better. At more advanced levels, these applications will follow tempo and dynamic changes of the performer, giving a more musical accompaniment as students add more advanced phrasing and musical nuance to their performances.

Teachers need to know how to integrate these practice tools into their curriculum, and to guide students in better use of them in their personal practice sessions. Teachers should also learn to integrate these practice tools with music notation and sequencing programs, to create additional materials for student practice, more closely aligned with the school's curriculum.

The Internet has a wealth of materials for use in these practice programs, and teachers should develop bookmark sets for sites that provide good materials for their teaching. There are sites that offer thousands of Standard MIDI Files that may be legally downloaded. These may be imported into accompaniment software or sequencers for use in practice.

The Internet is also an invaluable collection of online learning materials. While not organized as such, the Internet can become a library-like destination for music learning. Teachers need to develop strategies for integrating this resource into their classrooms, and also need to be able to guide students as they develop their own search strategies to augment independent research and learning.

There is an exciting project in process in Vermont. Middle and high school students upload their original compositions in Standard MIDI File (SMF) format for criticism and advice from teachers across the country. This is just one example of the extraordinary possibilities for information exchange via the Internet for music education.

Teachers must understand the various protocols used in connecting computers to the Internet, how to share files between computers of varying platforms, and be able to effectively search and retrieve information. Teachers should encourage students to use the Internet to find answers and to become life-long learners beyond the classroom experience.

Students can use this vast information resource to research any topic. Many libraries, both public and private, allow students to search their catalogs online and will give them the references requested.

**Multimedia**

Multimedia is the integration of sound, text, graphics, pictures, and video in a digital format. Just as computers may be used to store and manipulate MIDI performance and music notation, they may also be used to create, manipulate, and combine various media objects such as audio, video, and graphics. Incorporating these media elements into interactive computer environments provides a rich educational resource to support music instruction. This combination of multimedia environments is in and of itself a new art form.

There are many commercially available multimedia-based learning programs, distributed on CD-ROM, DVD, or via the Internet. For example, the music of Beethoven can be brought to life when the student can see a picture of the composer, read about his life and times, hear his music, and see a video performance from a concert. Teachers should know basic multimedia authoring strategies, to create materials for use in their classes. Perhaps even more importantly, teachers should be able to guide their students in learning multimedia authoring as they gather materials from Internet research and compile them into media rich reports. These reports may take the form of slide show presentations from computer, electronic portfolios, or Internet web sites.

To best support these strategies, teachers need to know how to record and edit sound, capture video, and acquire images from digital cameras or by scanning from print pictures. There are many technical issues in creating and manipulating these media elements. To transfer information from the real world (analog domain) into the virtual world (digital domain), information must be captured and digitized. This is usually accomplished through some form of analog to digital conversion technique.

Graphics may be digitized using either digital cameras or scanners that convert images into a collection of numbers called pixels (picture elements). Each pixel is a dot on the computer screen and represents one of up to a million possible colors. Each color is identified by its own discreet number. When digitizing video, a complete screen of pixels must be captured every thirtieth of a second in order to produce the thirty frames per second quality common to analog video.

In the digitization process of any media type there are always tradeoffs because image, sound, and motion quality is based on the amount of memory, storage, and processing power of the computer. To successfully work with digitized media, teachers must understand how computers process data, how data is stored and retrieved from disk, and how to balance sample or frame rate, bit resolution, data transfer rates, data compression schemes, and the various file formats in which digital media can be stored. Teachers need to know how to use the various editing tools available for digital media and how to edit and process media file types. Teachers must also learn to use various tools that allow files in one format to be converted to another so that files can be

---

combined into multimedia authoring environments. At the advanced levels, teachers should be able to use authoring tools which allow them to integrate digital audio, video, graphics, and text into a single document which can enrich various musical activities.

Strategies for digitization, editing, storage, and distribution of electronic media have become necessary skills for the twenty-first century teacher. Teachers also need to know how to combine these media into meaningful learning experiences for students. Perhaps even more important is helping students learn to express themselves in this new media, as a literacy requirement for their future.

**Productivity Tools, Classroom and Lab Management**

Computers are tools for creating, editing, and storing information or data in digital form. All computers have a microprocessor, varying by make or model, which carries out instructions and processes information; temporary memory dedicated to work space called Random Access Memory (RAM); a storage device such as a diskette, hard disk, or removable media; some output devices like a monitor, LCD display, or printer; and a few input devices such as a keyboard, mouse, trackball or trackpad, numeric keypad, or joystick used to enter information or select options from a menu.

Every computer has an operating system. This is software that determines how the computer will function, and what software it can run. Current operating system platforms include the MacOS (a version of Unix that runs on Apple Macintosh computers), Windows, and Unix (working on Intel-based computers). The data is stored in files, as determined by the software being used. There are a number of standard file formats that may be transported between software programs. Some of these are text for word processing information; .wav or .aif for digital audio; .mov or .avi for digital video; .gif, .jpeg or .pict for compressed graphic images, and .mid for MIDI files.

In addition to the value that it brings to the learning process, a computer can help the instructor to become more effective at managing the work of being a teacher. Managing a technology facility, be it a single computer and MIDI workstation in a classroom or a full music technology multi-station lab, requires specific administrative and management abilities. Teachers should understand the basic functionality of the personal computer, the various input and output peripherals usually connected to a central processing unit (CPU), and the variety of media used to store, transport, and retrieve information. Teachers should also have a working knowledge of the basic software tools used to manage a music program.

Word Processing software allows entering, editing, formatting, and printing of text-based documents. This is a helpful tool for creating concert programs, class handouts, tests, and various other office-related documents. Database software can be used to store and retrieve records for instrument and music inventories, class lists, attendance, and grades. Spreadsheet programs assist with the management of data including budget management, bookkeeping, or grades.

Graphics programs help even novice artists integrate illustrations into classroom presentations or word processing documents. Presentation software can be used to create overhead transparencies and slides for class lectures, or for presentations made to administrators, funding agencies, and parent groups. Personal Information Management (PIM) programs allow teachers to schedule rehearsals, meetings, and concerts, and to print customized calendars for students and parents.

Teachers should be able to install and run various applications programs and enter data, format pages, and print out reports. Teachers can use these tools to manage class activities and lab systems. In a shared facility, or in a classroom with a single workstation, it becomes necessary to keep hard drives free of student files and excess software applications, and to protect against computer viruses. Teachers need to understand these issues and develop strategies for maintaining their facilities in a manner that ensures effective use of the workstations while accomplishing their program needs and the goals of their curriculum.

Teachers also need to understand the way that multiple systems work together in a networked lab environment, and how audio, MIDI, and computer data is managed and distributed between systems. Many schools now provide networked server computers on which teachers may store classroom materials, and where students may post assignments for review. Today's teachers must understand how these systems work to most effectively use them in support of better teaching and learning.

At more advanced levels, teachers should be able to specify equipment needs for their classroom or lab facilities, understand the interaction and configurations for electronic instruments, computers, MIDI interfaces, sound reinforcement, projection systems, and sound and data networking. The more teachers know about these issues, the better prepared they will be to effectively integrate and manage music technology installations.

# SECTION 3:
# THE NATIONAL STANDARDS
# FOR ARTS EDUCATION

Tom Rudolph, TI:ME President, Haverford School District

This publication is based upon the work of the Music Educators National Conference and the development of National Standards for Arts Education, grades K-12 in the field of music. The goal of the *Technology Institute for Music Educators* (TI:ME) is to link technology and its many applications to the National Standards for Arts Education. The information that follows is largely an excerpt from *The School Music Program: A New Vision* © 1994 Music Educators National Conference, Reston, VA.[1]

## Background

In January 1994, the National Committee for Standards in the Arts announced America's first national voluntary standards for K-12 arts education. The standards were published as the *National Standards for Arts Education*. They represent the consensus of organizations and individuals representing educators, parents, artists, professional associations in education and the arts, public and private educational institutions, philanthropic organizations, and leaders from government, labor, and industry. The project was supported by the United States Department of Education, the National Endowment for the Arts, and the National Endowment for the Humanities.

The publication *The School Music Program: A New Vision* is intended for those interested in the quality of music instruction in America's schools. Its three main purposes are creating a coherent vision of what it means to be educated in music; building a foundation for a comprehensive and sequential curriculum in music; and providing specific assistance to improve the music curriculum.

---

[1] Excerpts from *The School Music Program: A New Vision,* copyright, 1994, by Music Educators National Conference (MENC). Reproduced with permission. Not for further reproduction without written permission from MENC. The complete National Arts Standards and additional materials related to the Standards are available from Music Educators National Conference, 1806 Robert Fulton Drive, Reston, VA 20191 (telephone: 800-336-3768)

**Categories of Learning**

The publication identifies the need for developing a new music curriculum for the twenty-first century. There are several distinct differences between this approach and the traditional curriculum. Many of these differences fall in the following seven categories:

1. Skills and knowledge as objectives: The music curriculum should be viewed as a well-planned sequence of learning experiences leading to clearly defined skills and knowledge, not as a random collection of student activities.
2. Diverse genres and styles of music: The music studied should reflect the multi-musical diversity of America's pluralistic culture.
3. Creative skills: The curriculum for every student should include improvisation and composition.
4. Problem solving and higher-order thinking skills: The curriculum should emphasize problem solving and higher-order thinking skills.
5. Interdisciplinary relationships: Ultimately all educational outcomes must cut across subject-matter fields in order to be useful.
6. Technology: The curriculum should use current technology to individualize and expand music learning. Through the use of computers, electronic instruments, compact discs, CD-ROMs, and various MIDI devices, every student can be actively involved in creating, performing, listening to, and analyzing music. Computers in particular can be used to facilitate the learning of basic skills and information. Teachers should work with students toward higher-level learning. Digital techniques make sound reproduction of the highest quality available in every classroom, while musical scores and resource materials also are quickly accessible. The technological limitations of the past have largely been erased. Advances in computer communications make possible the sharing of learning beyond school, state, and national boundaries.
7. Assessment: Every school district should develop reliable and valid techniques for assessing student learning in music.

Of the items above, number six, is especially relevant to TI:ME. Technology is the focus of the organization, but technology should be used for the enhancement and achievement of musical objectives.

**The Nine National Standards**

The National Standards for music include nine specific areas. These are shown below:

1. Singing, alone and with others, a varied repertoire of music.
2. Performing on instruments, alone and with others, a varied repertoire of music.
3. Improvising melodies, variations, and accompaniments.
4. Composing and arranging music within specified guidelines.
5. Reading and notating music.
6. Listening to, analyzing and describing music.
7. Evaluating music and music performances.
8. Understanding relationships between music, the other arts, and disciplines outside the arts.
9. Understanding music in relation to history and culture.

These standards are designed to reflect a national consensus concerning the highest priority skills and knowledge students should have acquired upon exiting grades 4, 8, and 12. They apply to every student through grade 8 and to every student enrolled in music beyond grade 8. Although music instruction in school is important in the development of those students who are talented in music, its primary purpose is to improve the quality of life for all students by developing their capacities to participate fully in their musical culture.

Each standard can be considered a broad content area. Within each content standard several achievement standards specify desired levels of attainment or explain how students will demonstrate their attainment of the desired level. The determination of the curriculum and the instructional activities designed to achieve the standards are the responsibility of states, local school districts, and individual teachers.

**The Achievement Standards**

Each of the nine content standards has several achievement standards. These are organized as K-4, 5-8, and 9-12 proficient and 9-12 advanced. For example, the achievement standards for content standard number 1, *Singing, alone and with others, a varied repertoire of music,* are listed below. There are separate categories for K-4, 5-8, and 9-12.

Grades K-4 Achievement Standards:

    1a. Students sing independently, on pitch and in rhythm, with appropriate timbre, diction, posture, and maintain a steady tempo.
    1b. Students sing expressively, with appropriate dynamics, phrasing, and interpretation.
    1c. Students sing from memory a varied repertoire of songs representing genres and styles from diverse cultures.
    1d. Students sing ostinatos, partner songs, and rounds.
    1e. Students sing in groups, blending vocal timbres, matching dynamic levels, and responding to the cues of a conductor.

Grades 5-8 Achievement Standards:

    1a. Students sing accurately and with good breath control throughout their singing ranges, alone and in large and small ensembles.
    1b. Students sing with expression and technical accuracy a repertoire of vocal literature with a level difficulty of 2, on a scale of 1 to 6, including some songs performed from memory.
    1c. Students sing music representing diverse genres and cultures, with expression appropriate for the work being performed.
    1d. Students sing music written in two and three parts.
    1e. Students who participate in a choral ensemble sing with expression and technical accuracy a varied repertoire of vocal literature with a level difficulty of 3, on a scale of 1 to 6, including some songs performed from memory.

Grades 9-12 Achievement Standards:

    1a. Students sing with expression and technical accuracy a large and varied repertoire of vocal literature with a level of difficulty of 4, on a scale of 1 to 6, including some songs performed from memory.
    1b. Students sing music written in four parts, with and without accompaniment.
    1c. Students demonstrate well-developed ensemble skills.

The complete achievement standards developed by MENC are listed in the publication *National Standards for The Arts,* available from MENC or by visiting their world wide web site at http://www.menc.org/publication/books/standards.htm.

**The Technology Areas of Competency and the National Standards**

The areas of technology are listed and defined in Section 2 of this document. The six areas are shown below:

1. Electronic Musical Instruments (INST)
   a. Keyboards
   b. Controllers (Other)
   c. Synthesizers and Samplers
   d. Ensemble Performance
2. Music Production (MUSPROD)
   a. Data Types
      i. MIDI
      ii. Digital Audio
   b. Processes
      i. Sequencing
      ii. Looping
      iii. Signal Processing
      iv. Sound Design
3. Music Notation Software (NOTE)
4. Technology-Assisted Learning (CAI)
   a. Instructional Software
   b. Accompaniment/Practice Tools
   c. Internet-based Learning
5. Multimedia (MULTI)
   a. Multimedia Authoring
      i. Web Pages
      ii. Presentations (PowerPoint, Keynote)
      iii. Movie/DVD
   b. Digital Image Capturing (Scanning, Still/Video Camera)
   c. Internet
   d. Electronic Portfolios
6. Productivity Tools, Classroom and Lab Management (TOOLS)
   a. Productivity Tools (Text Editor, Spreadsheet, Database, etc.)
   b. Computer Systems (CPU, I/O Devices, Storage Devices/Media, etc.)
   c. Lab Management Systems (Group Practice Systems.)
   d. Networks (Network Manager Software, Server, etc.)

In Sections 4 and 5 of this publication these areas are integrated with each of the nine National Standards for Arts Education. Technology areas one through five were written for both students and teachers. Area six, Productivity Tools, Classroom and Lab Management, refers only to teacher skills and competencies.

## Opportunity-to-Learn Standards for Music Technology

Immediately following the release of the National Standards for Music Education in 1994, MENC (http://www.menc.org) released Opportunity-to-learn Standards for Music Education as a guide to what schools should provide to help students achieve the National Standards for Music Education. MENC recommends that states adopt these Opportunity-to-Learn standards or use them as a basis for developing their own. The Opportunity-to-Learn standards for music technology are organized into four distinct areas:

- Curriculum and Scheduling
- Staffing, Equipment
- Materials/Software
- Facilities

The areas above are divided into lists that include minimal and desirable recommendations. For example, under the heading *Staffing for ages 1-5 or 1-6* are six minimal recommendations and an additional three that are desirable, one of which is as follows:

A planned program of ongoing staff development to provide teachers with training in applying technology in the curriculum is in place. Training is available on a variety of levels to match the varying backgrounds and proficiency of teachers.

There are additional recommendations listed in numbers 2-6. Under Desirable, there are three additional recommendations. One of which is as follows:

Music teachers have ready access to Internet-based professional development opportunities.

A copy of the Opportunity-to-learn Standards for Music Technology can be viewed and printed online. The complete version of the document can be viewed and printed from the web location, http://www.menc.org/publication/books/techstan.htm. MENC allows educators to print the standards from the web site and asks for a contribution for the publication.

The Opportunity-to-learn Standards for Music Technology contains helpful recommendations for teachers and administrators. TI:ME suggests that teachers purchase or download a copy and use it to review their program. The document can be helpful when budgeting for technology.

*References*

Music Educators National Conference, (1994). *The School Music Program: A New Vision*. Reston, VA: Music Educators National Conference (MENC).

National Standards for the Arts, (1992-1994). retrieved Jan. 23, 2005, from *MENC, The National Association for Music Education* Web site: http://www.menc.org/publication/books/standards.htm.

Opportunity-to-Learn Standards for Music Technology, (1999). retrieved Jan. 23, 2005, from *MENC, The National Association for Music Education* Web site: http://www.menc.org/publication/books/techstan.htm.

Music Educators National Conference, 1806 Robert Fulton Drive, Reston, VA 20191 (telephone:  800-336-3768)

# SECTION 4:
# STANDARDS OF THE
# INTERNATIONAL SOCIETY
# FOR TECHNOLOGY IN EDUCATION

Kim Walls, Auburn University
Bill Bauer, Case Western Reserve University
Floyd Richmond, Valley Forge Christian College

## Introduction

The International Society for Technology in Education (ISTE) is a professional organization for education technology leaders. One of the initiatives of ISTE is the National Educational Technology Standards (NETS) Project. According to ISTE's web site the purpose of NETS is

> to enable stakeholders in PreK-12 education to develop national standards for educational uses of technology that facilitate school improvement in the United States. The NETS Project will work to define standards for students, integrating curriculum technology, technology support, and standards for student assessment and evaluation of technology use. (http://cnets.iste.org/)

To that end, ISTE has collaborated with a variety of other educational technology organizations and teacher accreditation agencies to develop technology standards for students, teachers, administrators, and university teacher preparation programs. Nearly every state educational agency has adopted or adapted ISTE's standards for assessment of students, teachers, administrators, and/or teacher training institutions. In addition to developing standards, ISTE publishes information that describes effective uses of technology in teaching and learning. ISTE is developing materials that detail essential support systems for integrating technology into learning as well as materials for assessing student technology growth and evaluating the uses of technology in learning environment.

**NETS-S**

ISTE's National Educational Technology Standards for Students are also known as NETS-S. In 1998, ISTE published The Technology Foundation Standards for Students. The Foundation Standards are divided into six categories:

1. Basic operations and concepts
2. Social, ethical, and human issues
3. Technology productivity tools
4. Technology communications tools
5. Technology research tools
6. Technology problem-solving and decision-making tools

Each of the categories are further developed in ISTE's Profiles for Technology Literate Students which has Performance Indicators for four levels of students: Grades PreK - 2, Grades 3 - 5, Grades 6 - 8, and Grades 9 - 12. Each level has ten performance indicators that are cross-referenced with the Foundation Standards.

**NETS-T**

NETS-T are the ISTE standards which identify what teachers need to know and be able to do to effectively use technology in their teaching. The standards have six categories that are cross-referenced with the NETS-T Performance Indicators:

1. Technology operations and concepts
2. Planning and Designing Learning Environments and Experiences
3. Teaching, Learning, and the Curriculum
4. Assessment and Evaluation
5. Productivity and Professional Practice
6. Social, Ethical, Legal, and Human Issues

The NETS-T Performance Indicators are divided into three levels for preservice teachers: those completing their (a) general university preparation, (b) professional education courses, and (c) the student teaching internship). The fourth level of NETS-T Performance indicators is for first-year teachers. Since the principal accrediting agency for teacher education programs, NCATE, has adopted ISTE's recommendations, many preservice teachers are receiving the training they need to integrate technology into their teaching. Since most education agencies expect teachers to meet standards based on

NET-T, veteran teachers may find themselves needing training such as TI:ME courses to meet the teacher technology standards for their school districts or state departments of education. Teachers will also need to address NETS-S standards with their students. TI:ME courses could help music teachers to be an integral part of the process of integrating technology across the curriculum.

## NETS-A

ISTE collaborated with a variety of educational and professional organizations and training institutions in the Technology Standards for School Administrators (TSSA) Collaborative to develop the National Educational Technology Standards for Administrators. The standards were written for three types of administrators: superintendent and executive cabinet, district-level leaders for content-specific or other district programs, and campus-level leaders including principals and assistant principals. The standards are divided into the following categories:

1. Leadership and Vision,
2. Learning and Teaching,
3. Productivity and Professional Practice,
4. Support, Management, and Operations,
5. Assessment and Evaluation, and
6. Social, Legal, and Ethical Issues.

## TI:ME Strategies and the ISTE Standards

Each NETS-S grade level and each NETS-T teacher preparation level has its own set of performance indicators. Each performance indicator is related to one or more of the six categories for that set of standards. The TI:ME strategies for students and teachers can contribute to students meeting the NETS-S performance indicators and teachers demonstrating the NETS-T performance indicators. The ways that music teachers implement TI:ME strategies in their classrooms and rehearsals influence whether or not progress is made toward the NETS-S and NETS-T standards. By keeping in mind the student and teacher NETS categories when planning and implementing TI:ME strategies learning experiences, music teachers can create an environment where they and their students meet the ISTE standards.

| Students | Teachers |
|---|---|
| 1. Basic operations and concepts | 1. Technology operations and concepts |
| 2. Social, ethical, and human issues | 2. Planning and Designing Learning Environments and Experiences |
| 3. Technology productivity tools | 3. Teaching, Learning, and the Curriculum |
| 4. Technology communications tools | 4. Assessment and Evaluation |
| 5. Technology research tools | 5. Productivity and Professional Practice |
| 6. Technology problem-solving and decision-making tools | 6. Social, Ethical, Legal, and Human Issues |

Table 1. NETS Categories for Students and First-Year Teachers

NETS Category 1 (see table above) is similar for teachers and students, advancing in depth of understanding across the grade levels to the teacher level. Any TI:ME student activity can meet both student and teacher performance indicators related to Category 1 because technology operations and concepts are being used any time students are engaged in music technology activities that have been designed by their teacher. As an example, in the TI:ME student activity "The student captures musical performances for self-evaluation or evaluation by the teacher using notation or sequencing software" the technology operations may be as basic as using the mouse to press the record button and the stop button in a sequencing program, corresponding to ISTE Performance Indicator 1 for Grades PreK-2. If the strategy was adapted for a high school student, the process of implementing the TI:ME strategy might include a discussion of why certain software tools are most appropriate for the compositional task. Teachers who planned and implemented the TI:ME strategy exhibited several Category 1 skills. They would have had to understand how to use and connect the software and the electronic instruments as well as making sure that all of the technological components were present and working. An understanding of the strengths and weaknesses of the possible choices in the software and choosing the best software is also related to Category I.

"Social, ethical, and human issues" related to technology is NETS-S Category 2 and NETS-T Category 6. Many of the TI:ME strategies may be implemented as small group student activities. In the student activity "The student demonstrates analytical and listening skills by crating a multimedia presentation on a composer or other musical concepts" students can learn how to work as a team as they collaborate as a group to create the presentation and share computers and other equipment. Students can learn how to use technology in a responsible and ethical manner by taking care of the equipment and following copyright guidelines. The teacher demonstrates ethical uses of technology by explaining and demonstrating adherence to copyright guidelines. The teachers also make certain that the assignment and activities are accessible to all students. For example, the teacher must account for the fact that not all students have the ability to search the Internet for media from their homes. Setting up the computer stations so that they are ergonomically appropriate for the students also relates to human issues. The teacher is careful to follow school policies and safe practices when displaying students' multimedia projects in public, such as on web sites, so that students' privacy is ensured.

NETS-S Category 3 and NETS-T Category 5 involve technology productivity tools. Any time that a student creates music with technology, develops multimedia, manages electronic data, or uses technology to report learning to others they are using productivity tools. Both the notation/music production activity and the multimedia activity described above involve the use of technology productivity tools by students. The teacher category "Productivity and Professional Practice" differs from the student category "Technology productivity tools" in that the teacher uses productivity tools for professional development and collaboration with professional colleagues and parents of students. An excellent example of a TI-ME teacher activity that addresses NETS-T Category 5 is "The teacher uses Internet services such as e-mail, list servers, and chat rooms for music learning." The TI:ME listserv and web site are excellent tools available for music teachers to collaborate and grow professionally in this manner.

Students' use of "Technology communications tools" (NETS-S Category 4) involves using technology to report what has been learned about music through technology and also using communication technology with others to learn about music. Any time that students share the products of their TI:ME learning activities with their class or people outside the classroom, they are working in Category 4. The TI:ME activity "The student exchanges information on music, history, and culture with other students throughout the world using the Internet" is a way that students can communicate to learn more about music. TI:ME Strategies in which students research music through the Internet or through music learning software are related to NET-S Category 5: "Technology research tools." Two examples are "The student researches information related to listening – such as musical style or historical information using the Internet" and "The student locates historical and cultural information using the Internet."

Creating music or multimedia involves solving problems and making decisions, so whenever a TI:ME activity requires students to create a project, NETS-S Category 6 is being met. Some music learning software strategies may also address Category 6 if the student is solving a music puzzle or problem in a software game.

NETS-T Categories 2, 3, and 4 of technology use, "Planning and Designing Learning Environments and Experiences," "Teaching, Learning, and the Curriculum," and "Assessment and Evaluation," are correlated with fifteen of the twenty-one Performance Indicators for teachers. These categories of technology use are concerned with the "behind the scenes" work of the teacher in implementing and assessing a curriculum through TI:ME strategies. For example, if one "looks behind the scene" of the TI:ME activity "The teacher conducts a chorus or class using a recorded (MIDI sequenced) accompaniment," both Categories 2 and 3 are assumed. The teacher should have purposefully chosen this activity because the goals of the curriculum are being advanced. The activity addresses national music standard 1 thereby meeting ISTE Category 2. NETS-T Category 3 is involved with designing learning settings that use "current best practices." Although many settings for integrating technology into learning are small-group collaborative activities, it may be argued that this TI:ME Strategy involving an entire chorus is a "current best practice" for the national music standard of "singing with others" using technology.

Category 4 is best represented in the NETS-T performance indicator which reads

use technology tools to collect, analyze, interpret, represent, and communicate data (student performance and other information) for the purposes of instructional planning and school improvement. (http://cnets.iste.org/teachers/t_profile-first.html)

Some of the data sources for assessment may be digital, such as results from music learning software tests or electronic portfolios. Assessment is explicit in many of the TI:ME Strategies. Other Strategies imply assessment in their possibilities for embedded assessment. Some of the explicit assessment activities include the following items.

- The teacher records and evaluates student performances using notation or sequencing software.
- The student captures musical performances for self-evaluation or evaluation by the teacher using notation or sequencing software.
- The teacher averages grades, tracks fund-raising projects and prepares budgets, using spreadsheet software.

The following strategies are just a few examples that can be used as data sources for embedded assessment:

- The student composes pieces demonstrating the ranges of traditional instruments using a notation program or MIDI sequencing software,
- The student self-evaluates music reading and notation skills using appropriate computer-assisted instruction software,
- The student writes a review or analysis of music using word processing software, and
- The student creates a multimedia presentation demonstrating the relationship of music to the arts and other disciplines.

## Conclusion

Both ISTE and TI:ME have provided a wealth of materials to assist music teachers in the appropriate integration of technology to achieve the National Standards in Music as well as the NET-S standards. In doing so, they are also demonstrating their own competence in the NETS-T standards. Each NETS Performance Indicator generally overlaps several NETS categories, just as most TI:ME Strategies span more than one NETS category and National Music Standard. The TI:ME Strategies Chart in Appendices A and B cross references TI:ME student activities and teacher activities with the most applicable NETS categories and National Music Standards. The Appendix should help music teachers apply TI:ME Strategies in a thoughtful manner, keeping the NETS-S and NETS-T categories in mind, so that music teachers can demonstrate the NETS-T Performance Indicators as well as help students demonstrate the NETS-S Performance Indicators.

*References*

*Articles*

Bauer, W. I. (2002). Technology Standards for Music Teacher Education. Retrieved April 21, 2004 from http://atmi2002.billbauer.net (Note: This will download a PDF file.)

Walls, K. C. (2000). Technology for Future Music Educators. *Journal of Music Teacher Education, 9(2),* 14-21.

Bauer, W. I. & Dunn, R. E. (2003). Digital reflection: The electronic portfolio in music teacher education. *Journal of Music Teacher Education, 13* (1), 7-20.

*Web Sites*

ISTE | Home (2004). retrieved Jan. 23, 2005, from *International Society for Technology in Education* Web site: http://www.iste.org.

International Society for Technology in Education National Educational Technology Standards, (2004). retrieved Jan. 23, 2005, from *National Educational Technology Standards Project* Web site: http://cnets.iste.org/.

Technology Foundation Standards for All Students (2004). retrieved Jan. 23, 2005, from *National Educational Technology Standards Project* Web site: http://cnets.iste.org/teachers/t_stands.html.

Educational Technology Standards and Performance Indicators for All Teachers, (2004). retrieved Jan. 23, 2005, from *National Educational Technology Standards for Teachers* Web site: http://cnets.iste.org/teachers/t_stands.html.

Educational Technology Standards and Performance Indicators for Administrators, (2004). retrieved Jan. 23, 2005, from National Educational Technology Standards for Administrators Web site: http://cnets.iste.org/administrators/a_stands.html.

Note: The web addresses found in this section are current as of the date of publication. See http://www.ti-me.org/technologystrategies/iste/ for updated links.

# SECTION 5:
# STUDENT AND TEACHER STRATEGIES
# AND ACTIVITIES

Tom Rudolph, TI:ME President, Haverford School District
Floyd Richmond, Valley Forge Christian College

Section 5 addresses technology areas one through six relating each to the *National Standards For Arts Education*. Each content standard is addressed in order with specific student activities and teacher strategies listed. Appendix A organizes these technology strategies according to the MENC Content Standards while in Appendix B they are organized by the six TI:ME technology areas.

Section 5 is organized as follows:

**Description:** This briefly explains the application of technology to assist in the achievement of the National Standards. It is meant as an overview, not a comprehensive listing.

**Listing of student activities in the area of technology:** These statements represent some of the possible activities for students in grades K-12 and are meant to be ideas for using technology.

**Listing of teacher strategies in the area of technology:** These strategies describe some of the ways technology can be used by the teacher to enhance various facets of music education. Teachers may choose to use some or all of the techniques as they apply to their individual teaching needs.

**Numbering System; 1.01, 2.03, etc.:** Each technology achievement activity and strategy is listed in numerical order. The first number (to the left of the decimal point) refers to the MENC Content Standard. The number following the decimal point is the individual technology standard.

**Appendix A -** Appendix A is a chart of the technology activities and strategies organized by MENC Content Standards.

**Appendix B -** Appendix B is a chart of the technology activities and strategies organized by the six TI:ME technology areas:

1. Electronic Musical Instruments (INST)
2. Music Production (MUSPROD)
3. Music Notation Software (NOTE)
4. Technology-Assisted Learning (CAI)
5. Multimedia (MULTI)
6. Productivity Tools, Classroom and Lab Management (TOOLS)

## Content Standard #1: Singing, alone and with others, a varied repertoire of music

*Student use of Technology:*

There are a variety of ways that technology can be used to enhance this standard. For example, some computer-assisted instruction (CAI) software is designed to evaluate the ability to sing on pitch. Other CAI programs are available to help students practice rhythms. CAI software can be used in a computer lab, in the classroom, or independently.

Multitrack music production software can also enhance singing by allowing students to alter the tempo, key, and timbre of a piece. With a MIDI sequencer, students can mute individual parts of a composition for more effective practice. Other specialized programs/devices are available for the vocalist. Some are designed to intelligently accompany vocalists in rehearsal and performance.

There are also many locations on the Internet where MIDI files can be copied to disk (downloaded) and used with a MIDI sequencer. Students can search for appropriate files and download them for use in rehearsal and performance. This can be especially helpful when singing songs representing genres and styles from diverse cultures.

### *Student Activities for Content Standard #1:*
1.01 The student improves pitch accuracy using computer-assisted instruction (CAI) software.
1.02 The student improves rhythmic accuracy using CAI software.
1.03 The student isolates individual parts for singing practice/rehearsal using music production and/or notation software.
1.04 The student practices singing one on a part using practice and performance devices.
1.05 The student searches for MIDI files using the Internet to use for practice.

*Teacher use of Technology:*

Using music production software or automatic accompaniment software, choral/classroom/instrumental teachers can create accompaniments in any genre. Music production software can easily control tempo and key. Parts can be muted for rehearsal and performance. Once an accompaniment is recorded or purchased, it can be used to free the teacher to conduct the ensemble. Students can then be expected to respond to the cues of the conductor. In addition, teachers can create accompaniment files that can be distributed to them on CD or via the Internet.

### *Teacher Strategies for Content Standard #1:*
1.06 The teacher plays accompaniments using music production software.
1.07 The teacher conducts an ensemble or class using a recorded (MIDI sequenced) accompaniment.
1.08 The teacher creates practice recordings for students and burns them to CD.
1.09 The teacher creates practice recordings (or MIDI sequences) and posts them on the school or music web site.

---

**Content Standard #2:** **Performing on instruments, alone and with others, a varied repertoire of music**

*Student use of Technology:*

Using a MIDI keyboard or a MIDI instrument controller, students can perform melodies, rhythms, and chordal parts. Electronic instruments are effective in small or large ensembles as well as in multi-station labs equipped with electronic instruments/keyboards. They provide an excellent performance medium for students.

Electronic instruments are capable of playing a wide range of timbres. Students can select a variety of timbres that evoke diverse genres and cultures. Students can use electronic instruments to perform simple and complex rhythm patterns using a variety of percussion sounds. Some devices are designed to be used by the instrumentalist in performance. These applications can accompany the performer in rehearsal and performance.

Using appropriate software students can use the computer to help learn to play a musical instrument. A number of programs are available which provide a series of sequential instrumental lessons. A number of others address aspects of music important to instrumental performance.

The Internet provides access to locations where MIDI files can be copied to disk (downloaded) and used with a MIDI sequencer. Students can search for appropriate files, download them, and use them for rehearsal and/or performance.

*Student Activities for Content Standard #2:*

2.01 The student performs melodic, rhythmic and chordal parts using electronic instruments.
2.02 The student performs one-on-a-part using electronic instruments.
2.03 The student learns to play an instrument using appropriate computer-assisted instruction software.
2.04 The student performs music of diverse genres and cultures using electronic keyboard/instruments and sound modules.
2.05 The student demonstrates the ability to maintain a steady beat using MIDI percussion controllers or electronic keyboards.
2.06 The student uses practice and performance devices in rehearsal and/or performance.
2.07 The student searches for MIDI files using the Internet and uses them for practice and performance.
2.08 The student composes using electronic instruments.

## Teacher use of Technology:

Using music production or automatic accompaniment software, instrumental, choral and classroom specialists can generate custom accompaniments. Using sequencing software, the tempo and key can be changed and parts can also be muted for rehearsal and demonstration. An electronic keyboard or electronic instrument lab can be used for solo and group performances.

### Teacher Strategies for Content Standard #2:

2.09 The teacher plays accompaniments using music production and/or accompaniment software.

2.10 The teacher selects appropriate music for students to use in live performance.

2.11 The teacher accesses General MIDI (GM) sounds using a GM instrument or sound module.

2.12 The teacher uses notation software to compose and print music for electronic instruments.

## Content Standard #3: Improvising melodies, variations, and accompaniments

*Student use of Technology:*

Electronic instruments can be used by students as tools for improvisation. They can provide a wide range of pitched and non-pitched sounds for use when improvising. Many electronic keyboard models come with built-in rhythmic and chordal patterns that can be accessed using one or two fingers. This can be a way for students to explore and compose harmonic progressions, melodies, and variations.

Accompaniment software can be used by students to improvise and record melodies and accompaniments.

*Student Activities for Content Standard #3:*

3.01  The student improvises melodic phrases and answers using electronic instruments.
3.02  The student improvises simple songs and compositions using a variety of electronic sound sources.
3.03  The student improvises percussion parts using an electronic keyboard.
3.04  The student creates original harmonic progressions using the "single finger" left hand bass function contained on many electronic keyboards.
3.05  The student uses auto-accompaniment software for improvisation.
3.06  The student records vocal improvisation using music production/digital audio software.
3.07  The student improvises jazz solos.

*Teacher use of Technology:*

Teachers can use the music production and intelligent software to create background tracks for improvisation. These can be played in rehearsal and performance aiding student improvisation. Teachers can use software to create custom exercises for student composition.

*Teacher Strategies for Content Standard #3:*

3.08  The teacher creates ostinatos and accompaniments for student improvisation using music production or intelligent accompanying software.

## Content Standard #4:  Composing and arranging music within specified guidelines

*Student use of Technology:*

Students can create (compose) original background sounds for classroom readings and dramatizations.  There are software programs designed to be used specifically by young children.  With these programs music can be composed using non-traditional means such as drawing lines to compose a melody.  Students can arrange a piece of music using music production software to change timbres.  They can also experiment with different combinations of sounds music production software to alter the elements and characteristics of the music.  Melody, harmony, rhythm, timbre, and form, can be isolated, changed, and elements such as *ritards*, *accelerandos*, and *crescendos* can be created and controlled.

Notation software enables students to compose or arrange for voices and/or instruments.  It provides a way to listen to a composition as it is being composed and print legible scores and parts.  Compositions using a variety of instruments and ranges can be enhanced by using notation software.  Students can play their compositions using a variety of timbres.  Notes can be entered in step time or real time.

Students can use software for editing and storing custom sounds.  They can create and edit sounds for their compositions and arrangements.  Some notation software has the built-in capability to manipulate music in many ways such as retrograde, inversion, augmentation, and diminution.  With notation or MIDI sequencing programs, music can be copied and pasted into other parts of compositions creating musical forms such as ABA, AABA, and Rondo.

With an electronic controller and sound source (module), sounds can be created, edited, and stored.  Some music production programs can generate time code used when synchronizing MIDI sequences with video and film.  This software can be used to compose music to accompany videos and movie soundtracks.  Using a MIDI sequencer with digital audio capability, sounds can be recorded and digitally edited for analysis or playback.

*Student Activities for Content Standard #4:*

4.01 The student creates effects to accompany readings and dramatizations using an electronic sound source (MIDI keyboard, MIDI controller).

4.02 The student composes original compositions using software designed for younger students or non-music readers.

4.03 The student changes the timbres of one or more parts in a prerecorded MIDI sequence.

4.04 The student demonstrates the elements of music using music production software.

4.05 The student manipulates audio and MIDI loops to create in original composition.

4.06 The student arranges pieces for various voices or instruments using a notion program.

4.07 The student composes pieces demonstrating the ranges of traditional instruments using a notation program or music production software.

4.08 The student records music in step time and real time using music production or music notation program.

4.09 The student creates compositional forms (ABA, Rondo, theme and variations, and so forth) using a sequencer or notation program.

4.10 The student creates, edits, and stores sounds using a MIDI instrument, a sound source, and editor/librarian software.

4.11 The student composes music using algorithmic composition software.

4.12 The student records a MIDI sequence and synchronizes it with a movie soundtrack, film, or video.

4.13 The student records and edits acoustic sounds using digital sound editing software.

## Teacher use of Technology:

Teachers can create musical examples with music production software. For example, a sequence can play every part with the melody muted. Students can then compose a melody over the existing sequence. When teachers create custom examples for students, the compositional process is enhanced. Teachers can also create musically expressive sequences using MIDI controllers. Quality sounding sequences can be used to teach beginning and advanced compositional techniques. Some MIDI sequencers allow for complex editing, mixing, and digital audio. These tools can be used by teachers to create exercises to help students compose and arrange music within specified guidelines.

*Teacher Strategies for Content Standard #4:*

4.14 The teacher creates multi-timbral musical examples using music production software.

4.15 The teacher creates musically expressive MIDI sequences using appropriate MIDI controllers.

4.16 The teacher edits and performs complex mixing processes, and integrates digital audio with MIDI sequences.

4.17 The teacher creates lesson plans for student composition by creating files for use with music production and music notation software that students manipulate to create their own compositions.

## Content Standard #5:  Reading and notating music

*Student use of Technology:*

Using notation software students can enter notes in step and real time on a virtual staff.  Music can then be played and printed.  There are also CAI drill and practice software titles designed to develop music reading skills.  Students can use this software to practice reading notes, melodies, and rhythms.

*Student Activities for Content Standard #5:*

5.01   The student notates music on a staff using notation software.
5.02   The student self-evaluates music reading and notation skills using appropriate computer-assisted instruction software.
5.03   The student will identify note names and rhythmic values using appropriate CAI software.
5.04   The student will solve musical problems requiring the mastery of sound and notation symbols using appropriate CAI software.
5.05   The student performs electronic instruments reading printed notation.

*Teacher use of Technology:*

Notation software provides teachers with tools to create musical examples for students.  They can be used for choral, instrumental and/or classroom activities.  Teachers can post notation files on the Internet for student practice and reference.

*Teacher Strategies for Content Standard #5:*

5.06   The teacher prints music reading exercises for students using notation software.
5.07   The teacher posts music notation files on the Internet using notation plug-ins for student practice and reference.
5.08   The teacher saves music notation files in a PDF format for posting on the Internet.

## Content Standard #6:  Listening to, analyzing and describing music

*Student use of Technology:*

Many computer-assisted instruction (CAI) software programs help students develop listening skills with exercises in contour recognition, intervals, rhythmic and melodic motives and error detection, major and minor chords, and chord progressions. Other CAI software focus on general listening skills.  Some programs guide active listening by presenting formal maps of the musical structure and organization while notation and commentary scrolls as the music plays.

Students can use the Internet to collect information about many aspects of music. Background information on composers and musical compositions are readily available. Some sites allow students to listen to musical excerpts in similar and contrasting styles.

Students can use a word processor to prepare reports.  With word processing software, music notation and graphics can be included in reports.  Using multimedia presentation or authoring software, students can create a project incorporating text, sound, and graphics.  This allows the synthesis of knowledge in many formats and sources.

*Student Activities for Content Standard #6:*

6.01  The student develops the ability to recognize and identify specific rhythmic, melodic, and harmonic elements of music using CAI software.

6.02  The student develops the ability to identify musical forms and recognize similar and contrasting sections using CAI software.

6.03  The student researches information related to listening such as musical style or historical information using the Internet.

6.04  The student writes a review or analysis of music using word processing software.

6.05  The student demonstrates analytical and listening skills creating a multimedia presentation on a composer or other musical concept.

*Teacher use of Technology:*

To select appropriate software for students, teachers should be acquainted with software designed to develop listening and analytical skills.  Word processing software can be used to create class handouts, tests, and other documents that can include notation and other graphics.

---

Teachers should be familiar with issues that effect recording, playing, and editing of digital media. This includes sample rate, resolution, compression, and transfer rates especially through DVD players, CD ROM drives, hard drives, and the Internet. Teachers should be able to open and convert files of various file formats including gif, jpg, wav, aif, mp3, .aac, mid, mov, avi, hqx, sit, and zip.

The Internet provides teachers with a tool to search and collect information. Using the Internet, teachers can find historical and stylistic information to enhance listening experiences and lessons. Also available are musical excerpts in digitally recorded and MIDI formats for use in classroom listening activities.

The computer can be used to present information to students. Screens from CAI, multimedia software, and the Internet can be displayed for class analysis. With multimedia authoring software, teachers can create listening lessons that use text, sound, graphics, and interaction to emphasize concepts. Because teachers can control the content of the lessons, the materials may be customized to the specific needs of the students.

With music production or accompaniment software, teachers can create listening examples. Because they can control entry and playback of musical examples, attention can be drawn to specific musical concepts. Using a MIDI sequencer teachers may turn tracks on or off to focus on the remaining voices. Teachers can re-orchestrate a section of a piece to demonstrate the effect of different timbres. Accompaniment software can change the style of a composition enabling students to listen and analyze and then describe what they have heard.

*Teacher Strategies for Content Standard #6:*

6.06 The teacher selects appropriate CAI and multimedia software to help the student build listening and analytical skills.

6.07 The teacher prepares a review or analysis of music for class handouts using word processing software.

6.08 The teacher creates and edits digital media (recordings, videos) for class presentations on listening using appropriate software and hardware.

6.09 The teacher researches information on music listening using the Internet.

6.10 The teacher presents interactive instruction and listening lessons to the class using the computer to display the information

6.11 The teacher prepares custom listening lessons for students using authoring software.

6.12 The teacher creates examples for students to listen to, analyze and describe using a MIDI sequencer or intelligent accompaniment software.

6.13 The teacher prepares a WebQuest for students that provides them with a tool to analyze and describe music of various cultures and genres.

## Content Standard #7:  Evaluating Music and Music Performances

*Student use of Technology:*

Some technology-assisted lessons, multimedia software programs, and Internet sites provide opportunities for students to evaluate music and offer recorded and MIDI performances of the same works which students can compare and contrast.  Internet sites can provide information about compositions that are being studied and/or performed.  Students may use these sites to collect information when evaluating music.  The Internet also provides access to music reviews and criticisms of performances and recordings.

Music production and notation programs allow students to record their performances using electronic instruments and digital audio.  These performances may be played repeatedly and at slower or faster tempos for more precise evaluation.  Music files created with music notation programs can be saved in a format appropriate for presentation on the Internet.  In these cases, students may view the scores in their browser using a plug-in.  Students may play the song and may change the key and tempo of the performance.  In some cases, students may save the file for further study.

*Student Activities for Content Standard #7:*

7.01   The student develops evaluation skills using technology-assisted-learning and multimedia software.

7.02   The student finds information to aid in the evaluation of music such as background, performance practices, and indicators of quality using the Internet.

7.03   The student uses the Internet to find and download multiple performances of the same work for comparison.

7.04   The student reads on-line reviews and criticisms of performances and recordings.

7.05   The student uses the Internet to research the history of music criticism and its impact on composition and performance.

7.06   The student captures musical performances for self-evaluation or evaluation by the teacher using notation or music-production software.

7.07   The student designs web pages and multimedia presentations which showcase his or her evaluations of music.

7.08   The student evaluates musical scores and performances on the Internet using a browser with an appropriate plug-in.

*Teacher use of Technology:*

Teachers should be familiar with instructional programs that help students learn to evaluate music critically. The teacher should be knowledgeable of software which provides exercises and examples for practice. The teacher should also be familiar with Internet sites which help strengthen skills in evaluation, and should be able to use the Internet to research information for related classroom lectures and activities.

The teacher may use music production software or intelligent accompaniment programs to create examples for students. The musical concepts and elements emphasized may then be customized to the specific needs of students. Music-production and notation programs allow teachers to record student and ensemble performances for evaluation. They may be played repeatedly for listening or at slower tempos for analysis. Music notation software may also be used to prepare scores for evaluation as they are presented on the Internet.

Using presentation and authoring software, teachers can organize musical excerpts into lessons which help develop evaluative skills. Once links to the musical examples are built into the lesson or presentation, excerpts may be played for students to critique. New musical examples may be added to the lesson o presentation as needed.

*Teacher Strategies for Content Standard #7:*

7.09 The teacher selects appropriate technology-assisted lessons and multimedia software to help students build skill in evaluating music.

7.10 The teacher finds background information, performance practices, and indicators of quality on the evaluation of music using the Internet.

7.11 The teacher finds multiple performances for students to compare using the Internet.

7.12 The teacher finds on-line review and criticisms of performances and recordings for student use.

7.13 The teacher finds Internet sites which describe the role and history of music criticism.

7.14 The teacher creates examples for students to listen, analyze, and describe using music production or notation software. The examples may be used within the notation software or posted to the Internet for viewing in browsers with an appropriate plug-in.

7.15 The teacher organizes and presents musical excerpts for students to critique using presentation or authoring software.

7.16 The teacher records and evaluates student performances using intelligent accompaniment software, notation or music-production software.

7.17 The teacher prepares scores for the Internet for evaluation by students.

7.18 The teacher designs web pages and multimedia presentations which help students evaluate music.

**<u>Content Standard #8</u>: Understanding relationships between music, the other arts, and disciplines outside the arts**

*Student use of Technology:*

Students can use educational software to help discover relationships between music and the other arts and disciplines. The Internet allows students to locate and collect information about the arts and other disciplines. Sites are available which display information about art, dance, theater, and the academic disciplines. Because the Internet includes text, sound, graphics, and video, students may view paintings, ballet and dance performances, operatic and theatrical performances, and listen to related music. Web quests in which the student is directed by the teacher to look for specific information on the Internet may be used to help the student make connections between music and the other arts and disciplines. A typical web quest might have the student design a circus act. To do so, the student must research circus music and hire a band, research elephants and buy them, and so on. As they use the web to solve these types of problem, students make connections to other disciplines.

Using multimedia authoring software students can create class projects and presentations. They can be organized to demonstrate how the arts and other disciplines relate to music.

*Student Activities for Content Standard #8:*

8.01 The student learns the relationship between music and the arts and other disciplines using technology-assisted lessons and multimedia software.

8.02 The student compares and contrasts two or more art forms from information gathered from the Internet.

8.03 The student creates a multimedia presentation demonstrating the relationship between music and the other arts and disciplines.

8.04 The student uses music production or notation software to create musical accompaniments for other art forms such as ballet, video excerpts, drama, and poetry readings.

8.05 The student uses Internet sites that use music to teach content from other disciplines including songs about the alphabet, math and grammar facts, states and capitals, historic events, the environment, and science concepts.

8.06 The student uses Internet sites which explain concepts from other disciplines which help understand music, its inner workings, its background, and its structure (science, physics, acoustics, engineering, recording, history, language).

8.07 The student completes web quests in which they research issues from the field of music and other disciplines.

8.08 The student designs web pages and multimedia presentations which show the relationship between music, the arts and other disciplines.

## Teacher use of Technology:

Teachers can use technology-assisted lessons that establish connections between music and the other arts and disciplines. Multimedia software and the Internet provide teachers with the means to research materials for presentation in the classroom. This information can be the basis for student projects which relate music to other arts and disciplines. Teachers should design web quests which direct students to make connections between arts and the other disciplines. Multimedia authoring software enables teachers to create projects and presentations.

### Teacher Strategies for Content Standard #8:

8.09 The teacher selects appropriate technology-assisted lessons and multimedia software that teach the relationships between music, the arts, and other disciplines.

8.10 The teacher collects materials which explain the relationships among music, the arts, and other disciplines using the Internet and multimedia reference software.

8.11 The teacher creates web pages and multimedia presentations demonstrating the relationships between music, the arts, and other disciplines.

8.12 The teacher uses music production or notation software to create musical examples to help illustrate connections between music and other art forms such as ballet, video, drama, and poetry.

8.13 The teacher directs the student to Internet sites which use music to help student learn content from other disciplines.

8.14 The teacher directs student to Internet sites which explain the connections between other disciplines and music.

8.15 The teacher designs web quests for students in which they research musical, arts-related, and non-musical topics.

## Content Standard #9:  Understanding music in relation to history and culture

*Student use of Technology*:

Many instructional software programs provide information about music and its relationship to history and culture.  Some software programs present music within a broad cultural and historical context.  Many programmable electronic keyboards and sound modules allow the user to alter and create custom tunings such as those used in the Renaissance and Baroque eras.

Because the Internet provides access to a wide variety of information about historical periods and cultures, students can use it to research class projects and papers.  They can also download and analyze MIDI and audio files from various cultures  for study using notation and music-production software.  Using the Internet, students can contact other students throughout the world via electronic mail.  Also, special newsgroups and web sites may be used to exchange information.

*Student Activities for Content Standard #9*:

9.01 The student learns to recognize relationships between music, history, and culture by using technology-assisted lessons.

9.02 The student creates various tunings on an electronic instrument to demonstrate the evolution of tunings throughout the history of music.

9.03 The student locates historical and cultural information using the Internet.

9.04 The student analyzes music of various cultures and musical styles using notation and music-production software.

9.05 The student exchanges information on music, history, and culture with other students throughout the world using Internet services such as chat and e-mail.

*Teacher use of Technology*:

Teachers should be acquainted with programs which present information about music and its relationship to history and culture.  Programmable electronic keyboards and sound modules allow the teacher to alter and create custom tunings such as those used in the Renaissance and Baroque eras.  Teachers can use standard MIDI files and notation and music-production programs to present music from various cultures and historical periods for listening, analysis, and evaluation.  Teachers can use multimedia software and the Internet to present materials to the class.  By using the Internet, teachers can contact others throughout the world via electronic mail.  Also, special newsgroups, discussion boards, and chat rooms can be used to exchange information with other teachers around the world. Teachers should also be familiar with how to create educational world wide web sites.

*Teacher Strategies for Content Standard #9:*

9.06 The teacher selects appropriate technology-assisted lessons and multimedia software to teach relationships between music, history, and culture.

9.07 The teacher creates various tunings using an electronic instrument to demonstrate the evolution of tunings throughout the history of music.

9.08 The teacher presents the music of various cultures and historical periods using notation and music-production software.

9.09 The teacher finds historical and cultural information for use in class using multimedia programs and the Internet.

9.10 The teacher collects and shares information about other cultures using the Internet.

9.11 The teacher designs web pages and multimedia presentations on the relationship between music, history, and culture.

Refer to Appendix A for a complete listing of all student activities and teacher strategies organized according to the nine MENC Content Standards.

See Appendix B for a listing of all student activities and teacher strategies organized according to the six technology areas defined in Section 2.

# SECTION 6:
# INFORMATION PROCESSING,
# COMPUTER SYSTEMS,
# AND LAB MANAGEMENT

Floyd Richmond, Valley Forge Christian College

This section is divided into three parts which support the accomplishment of the MENC standards through technology. **INFORMATION PROCESSING** identifies skills leading teachers to greater efficiency with paperwork, planning, and related tasks. **COMPUTER SYSTEMS** identifies skills required for the set-up, installation, and maintenance of software and hardware. **LAB MANAGEMENT** covers issues specifically related to computer labs and electronic instruments. These skills are useful to those who teach all ages and levels. Not all of these ideas, however, will be appropriate for every teacher. Teachers will apply the concepts which most address their individual needs.

## INFORMATION PROCESSING

Technology enables teachers to improve the quality and efficiency of many information processing tasks that they must complete each day. These tasks include writing reports and memos, averaging grades, keeping inventories, and maintaining one or more music libraries. As teachers become more efficient with these tasks, they are able to devote more time to instruction and planning. Specific skills described in this section include competency with word processing, spreadsheet, database, desktop publishing, graphics, presentation, authoring, marching band show design, and specialty or specific-purpose software.

### Word Processing:

*Information Processing Strategy 01:* The teacher creates letters to parents, memos to colleagues, and handouts for students using word processing software.

Word processors have powerful editing tools that check the spelling and grammar used in a document, suggest word substitutions from a thesaurus, and allow text to be easily moved from page to page. Professional quality word processing documents may

---

be produced using a laser or ink jet printer. Documents can be saved to electronic media in a fraction of the space required for equivalent paper documents and can be reloaded into the computer for further editing. Teachers should be able to write letters to parents, memos to colleagues, and handouts for students using word processing software.

Proficiency in the word processing software category requires the following skills:
1. Entering data by typing, scanning, or speaking
2. Saving and loading documents for further editing and use
3. Printing documents
4. Editing document contents by copying and pasting information
5. Operating the word processor's spelling checker, grammar checker, and thesaurus
6. Setting tabs and margins within the document
7. Incorporating graphics into documents

## Spreadsheet:

*Information Processing Strategy 02: The teacher averages grades, tracks fundraising projects, and prepares budgets using spreadsheet software.*

The spreadsheet is a time saving tool for record keeping. When mathematical formulas and calculations are required a spreadsheet may be used. Teachers should be able to average grades, track fund-raising projects, and prepare budges.

Proficiency in using spreadsheet software includes the following skills:
1. Entering data into existing spreadsheets by typing into cells, rows, and columns
2. Creating new spreadsheets including design, formula entry, and other calculations
3. Using the spreadsheet software to generate pie charts, bar graphs, and other graphic representations of the data

## Database:

*Information Processing Strategy 03: The teacher organizes class lists, keeps records on uniform and instrument inventory, and maintains a music library using database software.*

A database is a collection of specific lists of information. Database software can be used to organize and sort class lists, keep records on uniform and instrument inventory, and maintain a music library.

Proficiency with database software includes the following skills:
1. Entering data into records of an existing database
2. Creating a new database including all fields and records
3. Finding specific records using the database's search feature
4. Finding multiple records using the database's record selection or filter commands.
5. Generating reports such as mailing labels, form letters, and lists.

**Desktop Publishing:**

*Information Processing Strategy 04:* *The teacher creates newsletters and other documents using desktop publishing software.*

Desktop publishing software enables the manipulation of text and graphics. Teachers should be able to create newsletters and other documents using this software.

Proficiency with desktop publishing software includes the following skills:
1. Designing document layout
2. Entering data including text and graphics
3. Printing documents

**Graphics:**

*Information Processing Strategy 05:* *The teacher creates programs, concert announcements, and banners using general and special -purpose graphics programs.*

Graphics programs can be used to create documents for announcements and other publicity. Teachers should be able to prepare programs, concert announcements, and banners using general and special purpose graphics programs.

Proficiency with graphics software includes the following skills:
1. Designing documents
2. Adding graphics through drawing, scanning, and digital photography.
3. Editing graphics using the common tools of these programs (cut, copy, paste, rotate, resize, balance, brightness and color)
4. Adding and editing text and manipulating it graphically (adding shadows, embossing, and other effects).
5. Exporting and saving graphics in a number of formats for other programs.
6. Printing documents

## Specialty and Specific Purpose Software:

*Information Processing Strategy 06:* *The teacher uses specialty or specific purpose software (worksheet creation, calendar making, and grade averaging) as needed.*

Specialty programs are available for a number of purposes such as making music worksheets, creating calendars, and averaging grades. Although these tasks can be accomplished with other software, the specialty programs simplify the process.

Proficiency with specialty or specific-purpose software includes the following skills:
1. Selecting the appropriate software for specific tasks
2. Mastering the use of that software to accomplish the task
3. Saving, loading and printing documents

## Presentation Software:

*Information Processing Strategy 07:* *The teacher creates "overhead" materials for class using presentation software.*

Presentation software is designed to create and computer projected images, handouts, slides, and transparencies. Teachers can use this software for class lectures and demonstrations.

Proficiency with presentation software includes the following skills:
1. Designing a presentation
2. Entering text, graphics, and sounds
3. Presenting the project

## Authoring Software:

*Information Processing Strategy 08:* *The teacher creates custom technology-assisted lessons for students using authoring software.*

Authoring software can be used to create custom lessons for students. Teachers can personalize computer lessons and interactive assignments for classes. These lessons can be used in many educational environments.

Proficiency with authoring software includes the following skills:
1. Designing a lesson
2. Entering text, graphics, and sounds into the lesson
3. Creating screens incorporating student and computer interaction
4. Designing appropriate feedback
5. Incorporating student recording keeping

## Marching Band Show Design Software:

*Information Processing Strategy 09:*  *The teacher creates drill charts using marching band show design software.*

Marching band show design software is used to design and print out drill charts. By using this software teachers can save time, produce animations, and help students to better understand a halftime drill.

Proficiency with marching band drill design software includes the following skills:
1. Creating a marching band show including various forms and designs for the appropriate number of performers
2. Viewing the show from a variety of perspectives
3. Creating animations of the show
4. Adding music to the animation
5. Printing instructions for students.

## Internet and Telecommunications:

*Information Processing Strategy 10:*  *The teacher uses Internet services such as browsing, electronic mail, instant messaging, list servers, and chat rooms for music learning.*

The Internet connects many different types of computers:  government, academic, and commercial.  It can be used as a research resource for information on virtually any topic.  Internet services such as the web, electronic mail, and mailing lists, can promote music learning from diverse perspectives.  Students and teachers can exchange ideas and electronic discussions can be encouraged.

Proficiency with the Internet and telecommunications includes the following skills:
1. Using appropriate software including web browsers, helper applications, plug-ins, and utility programs
2. Searching for and finding information
3. Sending and receiving electronic mail (email)
4. Sending and receiving instant messages
5. Communicating using electronic mailing lists.
6. Using chat-room software

## COMPUTER SYSTEMS

This section identifies skills necessary for the set-up, installation, and maintenance of computers and electronic instruments. Specific skills to be covered include the set-up of peripheral devices such as hardware, audio and video equipment, printers, and external devices. Other considerations involve the installation and operation of computers and electronic instruments, and copyright compliance.

### Peripheral Audio Devices:

*Computer System Strategy 01: The teacher uses peripheral audio devices in a music technology lab.*

In order to be effective in a computer lab teachers need to operate peripheral audio devices such as tape recorders, CD and DVD players and recorders, and amplifiers. This will enable them to play music in a variety of formats and to record student projects as needed.

### Computer Components and Specifications:

*Computer System Strategy 02: The teacher lists and identifies the components of a computer system and can prepare a proposal for the purchase or upgrade of equipment.*

Many elements affect the performance of a computer. In order to select equipment appropriate for musical tasks, teachers need to understand processing speed, memory, and hard drive capacity. A knowledge of monitor resolution and color depth, printer resolution and color capabilities, CD and DVD recording and playback properties, modem and networking speeds, and audio and video capabilities are also helpful.

### Computer Installation:

*Computer System Strategy 03: The teacher connects and installs components of a computer system.*

Teachers should be able to set-up a computer, connect cables to the monitor, keyboard, and mouse, and install appropriate system, driver, and application software.

**Peripheral Equipment Installation:**

*Computer System Strategy 04:* *The teacher installs and connects peripheral equipment to a computer system.*

In addition to the computer equipment, teachers should be able to install and connect peripheral equipment to a computer system. This includes equipment such as printers, scanners, external CD and DVD drives, hard drives, modems, presentation hardware, audio equipment, video equipment, electronic MIDI instruments, and other devices as needed.

**System Software Installation:**

*Computer System Strategy 05:* *The teacher installs, operates, and troubleshoots computer operating systems (Windows, Mac OS).*

The efficient operation of a computer depends on the system software installed. This software manages memory, runs programs, and handles communication with the monitor, disk drive, and peripheral devices. Should the system software become corrupt, crashes are inevitable. Teachers should be able to install computer operating systems (Windows, Mac OS), correct problems, and set the system preferences for specific needs.

**Computer Security:**

*Computer System Strategy 06:* *The teacher installs software which limits user access to specific programs and data, thereby protecting the computer hard drive and system software.*

It is sometimes necessary to take steps to protect the computer from unauthorized tampering. Particularly sensitive areas are the system and application folders and the hard drive. Teachers should be able to install and operate programs which protect the computer from unauthorized access. The teacher should be able to operate the file sharing functions built into the operating system. This includes creating users and groups and assigning privileges for each computer.

**Virus Protection:**

*Computer System Strategy 07: The teacher installs and operates virus protection software.*

A virus is a computer program designed to corrupt data. It duplicates as widely as possible without permission. Viruses can spread over networks and online systems, through e-mail and on floppy disks which are carried from computer to computer. Some viruses are destructive. After reproducing themselves, they erase the computer's hard drive or otherwise interfere with the computer's operation. Even harmless viruses consume valuable system memory and storage space and may contain programming errors which could cause computer malfunction. Teachers need to take the necessary precautions to avoid damage to programs and files by installing and operating virus protection software.

**Internet:**

*Computer System Strategy 08: The teacher connects a single computer to the Internet.*

A growing number of resources are available over the Internet. Teachers should be able to connect a computer to the Internet. This includes selecting, installing, and configuring the necessary software (browsers, helper applications, plug-ins, utility programs); and selecting and installing the necessary hardware (modems, phone cables, network adapters).

**Copyright:**

*Computer System Strategy 09: The teacher is aware of copyright restrictions as applied to computer software and other files.*

Access to information is steadily increasing. The distribution of copyrighted materials is protected by law. Teachers should be able to list and define *the* fair use applications of the copyright law pertaining to hardware, software, and the use of files. They need to understand the copyright restrictions of commercial software, shareware, and freeware.

## Electronic Instruments Performance and Compatibility:

*Computer System Strategy 10:  The teacher can describe issues related to connecting electronic instruments for-performance.*

Electronic instruments have a variety of options which affect the way they are used.  Teachers should understand issues related to the performance and compatibility of electronic instruments including the quality and range of percussive sounds; MIDI and General MIDI capabilities; capacity for polyphonic, multitimbral and velocity-sensitive responses; built-in or external music production features; amplification; full-size and/or weighted keys; and availability of pedal controls.

## Electronic Instruments Set-up and Operation:

*Computer System Strategy 11:  The teacher sets up and uses electronic instruments.*

Electronic instruments must be correctly configured for proper operation.  The process is slightly different for each instrument.  Teachers should be able to set up and use electronic instruments; connect cables; select the various timbres; and use its unique features.  Teachers should be able to reset an electronic instrument to factory default settings when necessary.

## Multiple Electronic Instruments:

*Computer System Strategy 12:  The teacher sets up and uses multiple electronic instruments in performance.*

Electronic instruments may be combined to provide more alternatives in a lab or studio.  Sound modules add extra sounds to an existing keyboard or MIDI controller.  Instruments may be used in combination for greater harmonic depth.  Teachers should be able to set up and use multiple electronic instruments and sound modules with appropriate MIDI connections.

## LAB MANAGEMENT

This section identifies skills necessary for the set-up, maintenance, and operation of labs of computers and electronic instruments. These labs offer many advantages including increased educational opportunities for students, greater ability to exchange information and share resources.

### Design:

*Lab Management Strategy 01: The teacher designs the physical set-up of a computer lab and/or electronic instruments.*

Teachers should be able to design the physical set-up of computer and/or electronic instrument labs. Ergonomic considerations, including student comfort and traffic-flow, should be evident in the design.

### Network:

*Lab Management Strategy 02: The teacher uses appropriate software and hardware to connect computers to form a network.*

When computers are connected on a network, information and resources may be easily exchanged and shared. Teachers should be able to connect several computers to form a local area network (LAN) using appropriate software and hardware. This includes selecting an appropriate communication standard such as AppleTalk or Ethernet and installing necessary cards, cables, and software. Each computer station should be able to exchange files and use shared resources.

### Lab to Internet Connections:

*Lab Management Strategy 03: The teacher connects a computer lab to the Internet.*

Many educational benefits of the Internet are reached only when the Internet is available to an entire class. Students may then individually and simultaneously work on research projects, or view a teacher created list of sites at their own pace. Teachers should be able to connect a computer lab to the Internet. This includes selecting an appropriate Internet Service Provider (ISP) or working within an existing network, installing and configuring the necessary software (browsers, helper applications, plug-ins, utility programs), and selecting and installing the necessary hardware (modems, routers, hubs, bridges, fire walls, phone lines, network cable and adapters).

### Electronic Instrument Labs:

*Lab Management Strategy 04:* *The teacher uses appropriate software and hardware in a lab of electronic instruments to allow individual and group practice; to listen to and monitor student progress; and to lecture and perform to the entire class, individuals or small groups.*

When electronic instruments are connected using appropriate hardware and software the teacher may lecture and demonstrate to the entire class, explain and play for individual students or small groups, listen to students individually, and arrange for small ensembles to practice with one another. Teachers should be able to connect and configure such a system, and operate it properly.

### Budget:

*Lab Management Strategy 05:* *The teacher develops and maintains a budget for the purchase and updating of a computer/technology lab.*

The operation and maintenance of a computer and electronic instrument lab requires considerable planning including the development of a comprehensive budget for purchase and upkeep. This multi-year plan should include hardware (computers, electronic instruments), peripheral equipment (printers, scanners, modems), lab furniture, software and upgrades, staff training (materials, technical support), and repair and maintenance.

### Curriculum Development:

*Lab Management Strategy 06:* *The teacher designs lessons for use in a music technology lab.*

The selection and design of curricula are essential steps in insuring successful teaching and learning. The curriculum should take advantage of the unique resources offered by music technology. These include technology-assisted lessons. Internet research, multimedia development, creative projects which use electronic instruments, notation, and music production software.

# SECTION 7:
# ASSESSMENT AND MUSIC TECHNOLOGY

William I. Bauer, Case Western Reserve University

Assessment is a critical part of the teaching process. Music teachers use assessment for a number of formative[1] and summative[2] purposes including (1) to determine appropriate initial learning goals for students, (2) to decide if students are ready for the next learning experience or if remediation is necessary, (3) to consider whether specific topics or skills have been mastered, and (4) to establish the grades that students will receive. This chapter covers three aspects of assessment as they apply to instructional music technology. First, basic considerations in designing assessments will be reviewed. Second, assessment *instruments*, materials teachers use to document students' achievement of concepts and skills as demonstrated through music technology projects, will be discussed. Finally, selected technology-based tools that can assist teachers in assessing and grading students will be examined.

## DESIGNING ASSESSMENTS

Teachers must include assessment as part of the instructional design process. Grant Wiggins and Jay McTighe (1998) describe an approach that they label as "backward design" (p. 7) whereby teachers (1) identify what students should know or be able to do following the learning experience, (2) determine the evidence that will be acceptable in demonstrating student understanding, and (3) plan learning experiences and instruction. Wiggins and McTighe point out that teachers often start with the materials or activities of instruction (step 3) rather than developing lessons and curricula in the sequence outlined above. When designing learning experiences, as with many things in life, it is important to begin with the end in mind (Covey, 1990).

---

[1] Formative Assessment - Assessment results are used to adapt teaching and learning strategies to meet student needs.
[2] Summative Assessment - A judgment regarding the level of student achievement is made, as when assigning a grade.

Once teachers have determined what students should know or be able to do following a learning experience, they next need to decide how student achievement will be verified. Paper and pencil tests with multiple choice, fill in the blank, matching, short answer, and essay items are commonly used assessment instruments in the traditional classroom. When students are engaged in activities where learning outcomes include products or performances, paper and pencil instruments are not always the best means of determining what students have accomplished. Because of the unique characteristics of music technology projects, specialized assessment instruments appropriate for these activities must be developed.

It is essential that assessment instruments are *valid* and *reliable*. If an assessment instrument is valid, then it measures what it is intended to measure. For example, if students in band were given a test on the historical background of a piece of music they were performing, but the teacher had never provided the students with learning experiences on the topic, then the test would not be a valid measure of what the students had learned in class. Reliability is the consistency of measurement. To be reliable, an instrument should yield the same results, or score, if used at different times, assuming no further learning has taken place. Teachers should select or create assessment instruments that help them accurately and consistently measure student learning.[3]

To assess student products such as those developed when working with technology, three kinds of assessment instruments are extremely useful. These are (1) checklists, (2) rating scales, and (3) rubrics. While similar in some ways, the progression from checklist to rubric is one of increasing sophistication. The next section will outline the characteristics of these tools, and provide an example of each type. Also discussed will be the portfolio, an assessment instrument that can help the teacher achieve a broad understanding of students' comprehension of a subject.

**ASSESSMENT INSTRUMENTS**

Checklists, rating scales, and rubrics are all valuable tools. Teachers will determine which of these to use by considering exactly what they want to know about student learning, and the type of feedback they want to provide to the student and others.

---

[3] For more extensive information about validity and reliability in assessment, see *Measurement and Assessment in Teaching* by Robert L. Linn and Norman E. Gronlund (2000).

Students may also use checklists, rating scales, and rubrics for peer- and self-assessment. Let us assume that a teacher wants students to develop a more comprehensive understanding of a composer of their choosing. As outcomes of this project, the teacher wants the students to be able to describe biographical information about the composer, have listened to music by the composer, be able to list the composer's major musical works, place the composer in a particular style period and discuss the basic characteristics of music of that period, view a painting or photograph of the composer, and relate the composer's life to other events that were occurring in the world during the time period that the composer lived. To achieve this understanding, the students will use primarily, but not exclusively, Internet resources. To demonstrate their comprehensive understanding of the composer, the students will create a web page that addresses the various facets of the composer's life and music that the teacher has outlined.

Checklists:

Checklists allow the teacher to establish a minimum level for each competency or outcome and to indicate whether or not it was achieved. Beyond this, the teacher makes no attempt to rate the level of student achievement. A sample checklist for the composer web page project is found in figure 1. Using this form, the teacher would check the areas where minimum competency was achieved, and place a minus sign in front of areas where revision and further development was required.

| | Figure 1 Checklist for Composer Web Page Project | |
|---|---|---|
| | Content | |
| | Use of media (text, graphics, sound, video) | |
| | Layout and aesthetics | |
| | Writing mechanics | |
| | Technical aspects | |
| | Check mark (√) = acceptable,   Minus sign (-) = revision and further development needed | |

Rating Scales:

A rating scale is used when there is a desire to indicate not only the competencies or outcomes that have been achieved, but when the quality of the student's work also needs to be communicated. With this type of assessment instrument, a student receives feedback regarding the level of their achievement as measured on a scale. Figure 2 provides an example of a rating scale that could be used with the composer web page project. While rating scales let students know their standing on the items evaluated, they may not necessarily understand the criteria that were used to arrive at those ratings.

| **Figure 2** **Rating Scale for Composer Web Page Project** | | | | |
|---|---|---|---|---|
| Content | Poor | Fair | Good | Excellent |
| Use of media (text, graphics, sound, video) | Poor | Fair | Good | Excellent |
| Layout and aesthetics | Poor | Fair | Good | Excellent |
| Writing mechanics | Poor | Fair | Good | Excellent |
| Technical aspects | Poor | Fair | Good | Excellent |

Rubrics:

Rubrics, like rating scales, indicate a level of achievement. In addition to this, a rubric provides a short description of what the learner is doing when he or she performs at a certain level. These descriptors provide specific feedback to learners that can help them understand exactly what they are doing well, and conversely, what they need to do to improve. A rubric that might be used with the web page project is shown in figure 3. To learn about online resources that can assist teachers in creating rubrics, see the web page for this chapter at http://www.ti-me.org/technologystrategies/assessment/.

| Criteria | 1 | 2 | 3 | 4 |
|---|---|---|---|---|
| | | **Figure 3** | | |
| | | **Rubric for Composer Web Page Project** | | |
| Content | Understanding of subject is not well documented. Most content is unclear, inappropriate and/or incorrect. | Understanding of subject is not completely documented. Some content is clear, appropriate and/or correct. | Understanding of subject is somewhat well documented. Most content is clear, appropriate and/or correct. | Understanding of subject is well documented. All content is clear, appropriate and correct. |
| Use of media (text, graphics, sound, video) | No use of media other than text. | Minimal use of media. Some of the text, graphics, sound and/or video enhance understanding of the content. | Some use of media. Most of the text, graphics, sound and/or video enhance understanding of the content. | Extensive use of media. All of the text, graphics, sound and/or video enhance understanding of the content. |
| Layout and aesthetics | The layout is unattractive, disorganized, and/or cluttered. The background and colors are distracting and detract from the web page. | The layout is somewhat attractive, well organized, and uncluttered. The background and colors somewhat enhance the web page. | The layout is mostly attractive, well organized, and uncluttered. The background and colors mostly enhance the web page. | The layout is attractive, well organized, and uncluttered. The background and colors consistently enhance the web page. |
| Writing mechanics | The text has many errors in grammar, capitalization, punctuation, and spelling (more than 7 errors). | The text has errors in grammar, capitalization, punctuation, and spelling (5 or more errors). | The text has a few errors in grammar, capitalization, punctuation, and spelling. | The text has no errors in grammar, capitalization, punctuation, and spelling. |
| Technical aspects | Few links are functional, graphics do not display properly, and/or other media does not work correctly. | Some links are functional, some graphics display properly, and/or some of the other media works correctly. | Most links are functional, most graphics display properly, and/or most of the other media works correctly | All links are functional, graphics display properly, and other media works correctly |

Portfolios:

Portfolios are organized collections of student work that can provide a well-rounded portrait of a student's accomplishments. Portfolios have many potential strengths.

Because portfolios consist of products of classroom instruction, they can be readily integrated with instruction. Portfolios provide students with opportunity to show what they can do. Portfolios can encourage students to become reflective learners and to develop skills in evaluating the strengths and weaknesses of their work. Portfolios can help students take responsibility for setting goals and evaluating their progress. Portfolios can provide teachers and students with opportunities to collaborate and reflect on student progress. Portfolios can be an effective way of communicating with parents by showing concrete examples of student work and demonstrations of progress. Portfolios can provide a mechanism for student-centered and student-directed conferences with parents. Portfolios can give parents concrete examples of students' development over time as well as their current skills.[4]

Traditionally portfolios have been paper-based, assembled in file folders, binders, or some other appropriate container. More recently, electronic portfolios have come into use. These e-portfolios have been created with a variety of proprietary software programs and with html and other web-standard file types (Bauer & Dunn, 2003). Assembling music students' technology-based projects into a digital portfolio can be an excellent way for the student to demonstrate their overall understanding of subject matter and/or skill with technological tools in music. Depending on the number and size of files included in a student's e-portfolio, these records can be easily stored on digital media and/or relayed electronically to share with educator colleagues and parents. To learn more about electronic portfolio development, the reader is encouraged to visit the web page for this chapter at http://www.ti-me.org/technologystrategies/assessment/.

## TECHNOLOGY-BASED ASSESSMENT TOOLS

A number of software programs provide technological resources that can help the teacher with assessment and grading responsibilities. Many instructional music software applications are capable of automatically tracking student progress through the program's various lessons. Some of this software enables formative assessment of students through

---

[4] (Linn & Gronlund, 2000, p. 291).

games and electronic flash cards. These programs are frequently able to generate electronic reports documenting student progress that the teacher may print or save.

Other software applications make it possible for the teacher to develop customized quizzes in a variety of formats including multiple-choice, true/false, short-answer, jumbled-sentence, crossword, and matching question types. The quizzes created with these technologies can be administered via paper-and-pencil, on a computer, or online. In addition, free services for creating and hosting web-based quizzes may be found on the Internet. Such web sites often provide templates and simple-to-complete forms that require no specialized programming knowledge.

Grade book programs can assist teachers with the record keeping required to track student achievement. These programs are flexible and allow grades to be calculated using total points or according to weighted categories. Many also provide a means to track attendance. Grade reports can be printed or published to the Internet. More resources for using technology to develop quizzes and track student grades can be found on the web page for this chapter at http://www.ti-me.org/technologystrategies/assessment/.

## SUMMARY

Technological innovations are providing many new options for music teaching and learning. As teachers design learning experiences for students that involve the use of various technological tools, it is important that they remember the importance that assessment plays in the instructional process. By using assessment instruments such as checklists, rating scales, rubrics, and portfolios, teachers can fairly and accurately assess their students' understanding of subject matter. Finally, technology itself can help teachers with the assessment process. Software to develop various forms of quizzes and to keep track of student grades can make the logistics of assessment much easier.

## References

Bauer W. I. & Dunn, R. E. (2003). Digital reflection: The Electronic Portfolio in Music Teacher Education. *Journal of Music Teacher Education, 13* (1), 7-20.

Covey, S. R. (1990). The Seven Habits of Highly Effective People. New York: Simon & Schuster.

Linn, R. L. & Gronlund, N. E. (2000). *Measurement and Assessment in Teaching* (8th edition). Upper Saddle River, NJ: Prentice Hall.

Wiggins G. & McTighe, J. (1998). *Understanding by Design.* Upper Saddle River, NJ: Merrill Prentice Hall.

# SECTION 8:
# CREATIVE THINKING
# AND MUSIC TECHNOLOGY

Peter Webster, Northwestern University School of Music

## INTRODUCTION

It has never been a more exciting time to be a music teacher. As we plan strategies to involve our students in music learning, we do so at an unprecedented moment in our professional history when we see a confluence of new thinking both in and outside of music education. Certainly we remain committed to the notion that music represents a most unique way of knowing, an art form that touches us in ways that few other experiences can. However, the dominant view of music education as solely an aesthetic education has moved to a more synergistic position.[1] For example, conceptions of music teaching that have embraced only the Western concert music tradition have shifted to inclusion of more varied musics. Newer views of music intelligence and the role of creative thinking have challenged our more teacher-centered approaches.[2] The National Standards have added still more richness to our think-time concerning curriculum.

Changes in schooling itself have also occurred. A prevailing view on educational practice in recent years has supported a constructionist philosophy.[3] The basic goal of constructionism is to place emphasis on creativity and to motivate learning through

---

[1] For an excellent review of the changing landscape in music education philosophy, see Bennett Reimer, *A Philosophy of Music Education; Advancing the Vision*. Upper Saddle River, N.J.: Prentice Hall, 2003.

[2] More about this in Peter Webster, "Creative Thinking in Music: Advancing a Model. In T. Sullivan, & L. Willingham, (Eds.), *Creativity and Music Education* (pp. 16-33). Edmonton, AB: Canadian Music Educators' Association.

[3] One useful introduction to this perspective is Mitchel Resnick and Yasmin Kafai, (eds.) *Constructionism in Practice : Designing, Thinking, and Learning in a Digital World*, Mahwah, N.J.: Lawrence Erlbaum Associates, 1996.

---

activity. Learning is seen as more effective when approached as *situated in activity* rather than received passively.

Of course, music technology itself has developed greatly since the first days personal computing and computer-assisted instruction some twenty years ago. Development of music software that encourages creative thinking has allowed music teachers to guide students in creative tasks in ways never before possible. Programs for music composition, for improvisation, and for music performance provide extraordinary opportunities for teachers to encourage students to play with sound as they solve musical problems and act on their own creative ideas.[4]

Add to this the growth of the Internet. No longer is a teacher, a student, or a school an isolated set of entities, operating in a closed system. Some may site television as a technology that has effected change in education, but the computer and the Internet have far outdistanced television in its ability to deliver multiple forms of information on demand in ways that can be helpful to students as they work to construct their understanding of a subject domain with the teacher's help. The Internet has also provided methods of interaction and collaboration that have never before been possible.

It is in this context that we consider strategies for creative thinking with technology. The first set focuses on our own strategic planning as we teach music. Our end goals for our students are not always that they be generative, but—as we teach more skills and knowledge—*we can be creative*! The second set of strategies focus on generative student behavior.

## TEACHING CREATIVELY

How can we expect students to act creatively if we ourselves do not exhibit creative approaches to how we teach? Imagine how boring it must be for children to enter a music classroom, private studio, or rehearsal room and know exactly the routine that will always occur. Clearly there needs to be a sense of order and structure in classrooms, with established rules and boundaries, but teachers also need to create atmospheres that have change and a dynamic "edge" to the strategies. Students should have some sense of wonderment about what may be happening next. Technology can help with this edge and can really enliven the routine of learning. It can help us, as

---

[4] For a more detailed description of creative and other kinds of music software for computer-aided instruction, see David Williams and Peter Webster, *Experiencing Music Technology, 3ʳᵈ Edition.* Belmont, CA: Thomson Wadsworth, 2005.

teachers, feel more excited about the routines of teaching. Here are some suggested strategies.

1. **Electronic Kiosk**. What classroom does not have a computer lying around that still works but is too old to run today's software? One idea is to turn that device into an electronic kiosk that contains important messages that students can read when they come to class or walk by the teaching area. Using an old word processing program and large fonts, the computer can be used for announcements. Some software will animate the text. A student helper can enter the day's messages.

2. **MP3 Player for Audio Clips**. An mp3 player is a handy device to use in any music teaching to demonstrate an idea. Using a companion program, music teachers can digitize a wealth of personal owned music on their computer. Such devices, link easily to a room's sound system and playing examples in class from a number of pieces (planned or "on the fly") can be done quite quickly.

3. **Email Distributions**. An obvious way to use technology to help with instruction is by improving communication outside the teaching venue. Many students, even in grade school, have email accounts. Any standard email program will allow the creation of group email addresses. To help remind students of work or to clarify a point made in class or rehearsal, group emails can be used. Email messages can contain links to outside resources, including sound files that can be played on most computers.

4. **Course Management Systems**. Creating a website for a course or for an instrumental program and using it for instruction is always a creative way to support teaching. The idea of creating a custom website from scratch can be a daunting experience for some, so the use of course management system is a great solution for a school system. Course management software programs like *Blackboard* or *WebCT* are in common use in higher education, but more and more primary and secondary schools are beginning to use them as well. Mounted on a school system's central server, the management system allows teachers to create a website for a course without knowing any HTML coding. Teachers create course content by simply uploading files to the system. Students and parents can have immediate access. Students can submit work to a teacher for review in "digital drop" boxes and teachers can return work with

feedback. Sound and graphic files can be attached and exchanged as well and the site can be used in class as a place for saving work. Imagine how efficient it would be to have a course management site for a band or choir, using it to distribute practice materials and information about concerts and projects. Such management systems also include discussion boards to help with collaborative learning!

5. **Multimedia Support in Class**. A strategy that can enliven and help demonstrate musical ideas is to use a multimedia program. Often, a computer sits on a teacher's desk and is used only for administrative tasks. This same computer may have presentation programs installed. Hooking the computer to a projector or a large TV can create a visual display that can be effective in teaching. "Multimedia" is the use of three or more types of media used to teach an idea. When teaching about syncopation, the teacher can create a demonstration of how syncopation works with a music notation graphic, a small sound clip, and some text—all on the same screen. A series of these demos developed for class can be placed in a library for use in subsequent lessons and placed on a class website.

6. **Scores Displayed**. In a full band or orchestra rehearsal, players many go for years without ever seeing what a full score looks like. One way to use technology in rehearsal is to simply use an overhead projector with a transparency of the full score. Stopping the rehearsal for just five minutes to show students how the score represents the musical lines together can be a mind-opening experience for students. Such an approach can be combined with asking students questions about what they have been hearing and can make them more aware of issues of balance and blend. If this were accomplished with a computer as described in number five above, a number of possibilities for using sound and animation can be supported by the technology.

7. **CAI Software During Class/Rehearsal**. When do teachers have time to use ear training programs? One strategy is to have a small practice room or corner of a classroom designated as the "ear" area. Students can be randomly assigned to work with such programs during a rehearsal or a general music class—an internal "pull-out" system. Working alone or in teams, students can have a turn at using this important type of software on a rotating basis. If

done over a full year, the content of many of these programs can be experienced while still keeping a regular scheduled curriculum in place.

8. **Accompaniment Software in Class and On-line.** Today there are a number of computer programs which can be used to generate musical accompaniments in a variety of styles from a list of chords. Similar programs contain vast libraries of online accompaniments and can listen to the performer and follow them in time. These programs can be used in music lessons as background for etudes or as incentives for difficult passages. Any MIDI file can be easily posted on a website and played at home for practice. If the MIDI file is saved with separate tracks, a sequencing program can import the file and playback the music. Choral students can sing their parts with supportive accompaniment and voice parts.

9. **Recording an Ensemble.** Digital audio recording software can be used by ensemble teachers to record rehearsals as well as performances. Digital audio software can be used to record a portion of a rehearsal and then be used to immediately play the sounds for critical comment by the ensemble. The software can save the file as a compressed mp3 file and used later as a comparison to more polished performances. Such software can also be used by the student at home to show evidence of accomplishment with a digital portfolio.

10. **Performance Comparisons.** Digital audio recording software and mp3 players provide effective ways for students to hear contrasting performances. Critical listening is an important part of the National Standards and performance comparisons are excellent ways to develop strong listening skills. Much can be learned, for example, by comparing three different performances of a standard folk tune like "Danny Boy" or two interpretations of an early Beethoven symphony by a period instrument orchestra as opposed to the Chicago Symphony.

11. **Notation Software and Music Expression.** Standard notation software programs play obvious roles in music theory or composition classes for writing music, but what about their power to explore music expression? Such programs can playback sounds files with many different expressive styles, allowing students and teachers to experiment with not only note values but

*how* they are performed as well. Much can be learned about music by playing a non-expressive MIDI file as opposed to one that is crafted by a musician.

12. **Hand-held Devices for Record Keeping**. One final creative strategy is for teachers to use hand-held devices like a *Palm* or a *PocketPC* to help with data keeping. These devices can be programmed to keep databases on each student and the data can be uploaded to an electronic grade book on a computer.

## ENCOURAGING CREATIVE THINKING IN STUDENTS

But what about creative thinking for students? There are many examples in the literature of teachers using traditional software sequencers and notation programs to encourage students to compose or arrange music. Improvisation programs are used to accompany improvisational thinking in music. Often, these activities are done without much thought given to a specific strategy. Here are a few approaches that have a more defined focus.

1. **Etude/Scale Construction**. In a private lesson, have students use traditional notation software to construct their own etude that highlights a problem they are having. For example, if students are having difficulty with dotted eighth and sixteenth note rhythms, perhaps they could create an eight-bar melody with three examples of this rhythm. The notation program can play back the rhythm accurately and the student will have another model to use to hear the rhythm in a melody they created.

2. **Write a Rap**. Teams of students in a middle school general music class can be assigned the task of creating a rap using a loop-based sequencing program. One student can be in charge of words, another music, and a third can deal with movement if the team performs the rap. A general theme can be chosen for the raps, such as "Back to School," or "Learning Computers."

3. **Score a Film**. Writing film music is a great way to exercise creative thinking. Groups of students can be assigned the same film and final projects can be compared to see how each group handles the task. The Internet offers a number of sites that provide film clips that can be imported into sequencing programs. Students can use a MIDI keyboard to improvise sound tracks or to introduce digital sound effects.

4. **Experiment with Sound**. Much can be done with software and hardware to experiment with sound synthesis. Most MIDI keyboards have functions that support creating individual timbres. These are often not used by teachers and students because the built-in sounds are much easier to use. A great deal of knowledge about how sound works can be presented by using the hardware synthesizer's ability to alter sounds. Another approach is to use software-based synthesizers and samplers to create different sounds. Some programs include software resources that can be used to experiment with sounds. Virtual-studio programs also support extensive ways to alter and create new sounds using the sampler and synthesizer tools that are built in. All of these experiments with sounds can lead to timbres that can be used in original compositions. Finally, digital audio programs can be used to alter recorded sounds by adding digital effects such as reverb, normalization, and filtering of various types.

5. **Create a Mix of Analog and Digital Ensembles**. MIDI bands of one type or another are becoming more common. Teachers should encourage students to perform in more chamber music ensembles and forming an electronic ensemble to play traditional or original music is a great way to encourage creative thinking in music. Such activity occurs constantly outside of school, but way not inside of school under the expert guidance of music teachers? One strategy to encourage is the formation of ensembles that blend both digital instruments and computers with traditional analog instruments.

6. **Create Musical Toys**. An interesting strategy might be to have students create toys with MIDI sensors. MIDI sensors can be built very cheaply and added to tops like sponge balls or under carpets. The sensors can be used to trigger MIDI sounds and can provide a whole new world for creative performance.

7. **Listening *Blog***. *Blogs* are journals that are public and are often hosted on websites. They are designed to encourage communications on a particular topic—much like a discussion board. Since music engenders a number of deeply held perspectives, teachers can count on students to have strong feelings about particular pieces. One strategy that can be used to encourage students to think creatively about music is to create *blogs* based on common listening experiences. Music of all types could be hosted on a website and

students encouraged to enter their thoughts on certain aspects of the music. The *blog* might be expanded to include music and its relation to society and social messages.

8. **Keeping Digital Portfolios.** Related to number 7 is the notion of encouraging students to construct digital portfolios of their musical life. Such portfolios can contain their compositions, improvisations, listening *blogs*, and projects completed on the relation of music to other arts and music's social context. Such portfolios can be organized with CD or DVD construction software and can employ many different kinds of music technology.

9. **Multimedia Presentations.** Finally, a wonderful way to engage the imaginations of students is to encourage the creation of multimedia presentations on a particular music topic such as a style of music or a particular composer or artist. This can be done with multimedia presentation programs with and without interactive features. It can also be accomplished with web tools such as those associated with the WebQuest[5] model. The idea is to ask students to show evidence of their understanding of a topic by asking them to create a presentation about it. Students can be asked to use music software and hardware to do this. Such presentations can engage students deeply in the learning experience and can be great showpieces for parents to view.

Teachers using technology creatively and students using technology for creative thought can lead to powerful learning. Technology itself is meaningless if it cannot do something meaningful and each of these suggested uses should lead to positive results. It has never been a more exciting time to be a music teacher.

---

[5] For more information on WebQuests, see Tony Brewer, *WebQuests: The Secret to Guided Empowerment*, Eugene, OR: Visions Technology, 2004.

---

## References

Brewer, T. (2004). *Webquests: The Secret to Guided Empowerment.* Eugene, OR: Visions Technology

Williams, D., & Webster, P. (2005). *Experiencing Music Technology.* 3rd ed. Belmont, CA: Thomson Wadsworth.

Reimer, B. (2003). *A Philosophy of Music Education: Advancing the Vision.* Saddle River, NJU: Prentice Hall.

Webster, P. Creative Thinking in Music: Advancing a Model. In T. Sullivan, and Willingham, L. (Eds.), *Creativity and Music Education* (pp. 16-33). Edmonton, AB: Canadian Music Educators Association.

Resnick, M., & Kafai, Y. (Eds.). (1996). *Constructionism in practice: designing, thinking, and learning in a digital world.* Mahwah, NJU: Lawrence Erlbaum Associates.

# APPENDIX A

## Technology Strategies Organized by MENC Content Standards

The tables in Appendix A include the following information:

| MENC ACHIEVEMENT STANDARD 1 | TI:ME AREAS OF TECHNOLOGY | ISTE STAND | MENC ACHV STAND – GRADES |
|---|---|---|---|
| These refer to the nine MENC national standards for music. See Sections 3 and 5.<br><br>Student Activities and Teacher Strategies under this column are organized by MENC Content Standard. | These are the six areas of technology as defined by TI:ME. See Section 2. | These are the National Educational Technology Standards (NETS) of the International Society for Technology in Education (ISTE). See Section 4. | The information in this column refers to the MENC achievement standards for grades K-4, 5-8, and 9-12. There are one or more items listed such as 1a, 1b, etc. These refer to the MENC achievement standards that are most closely related to the technology strategy. |

The TI:ME technology strategies and related materials are available from TI:ME, 305 Maple Avenue, Wyncote, PA 19095 (telephone 617-747-2816).

The National Educational Technology Standards (NETS) of the International Society for Technology in Education (ISTE) and additional information are available from ISTE, 480 Charnelton Street, Eugene, OR 97401-2626 (telephone 800-336-5191).

The MENC achievement standards and additional materials related to the standards are available from Music Educators National Conference, 1806 Robert Fulton Drive, Reston, VA 20191 (telephone 800-336-3768).

See Appendix D for a summary list of these standards.

# TI:ME Technology Strategies

## Organized by MENC Achievement Standards

INST = Electronic Instruments; PROD = Music Production; NOTE = Notation Software,

CAI = Technology-Assisted Learning Software; MULTI = Multimedia; TOOLS = Productivity and Management

| MENC ACHIEVEMENT STANDARD 1 | | TI:ME AREAS OF TECHNOLOGY | | | | | | ISTE STAND | | MENC ACHV STAND - GRADES | | |
|---|---|---|---|---|---|---|---|---|---|---|---|---|
| NUM | STUDENT ACTIVITIES AND TEACHER STRATEGIES | INST | MUSP ROD | NOTE | CAI | MULTI | TOOLS | NET-S | NETS-T | K-4 | 5-8 | 9-12 |
| 1.01 | The student improves pitch accuracy using computer-assisted instruction (CAI) software. | | | | X | | | 1, 3, 6 | - | 1a | 1b | 1a |
| 1.02 | The student improves rhythmic accuracy using CAI software. | | | | X | | | 1, 3, 6 | - | 1a | 1b | 1a |
| 1.03 | The student isolates individual parts for singing practice/rehearsal using music production and/or notation software. | | X | X | | | | 1, 3, 6 | - | 1a | 1a, 1b | 1a |
| 1.04 | The student practices singing one on a part using practice and performance devices. | | X | X | X | | | 1, 3, 6 | - | 1a, 1d | 1a, 1b | 1b |
| 1.05 | The student searches for MIDI files using the Internet to use for practice. | | X | X | | | X | 1, 3, 4, 5 | - | 1c | 1c | 1a |
| 1.06 | The teacher plays accompaniments using music production software. | X | X | | | | | - | 1, 3 | 1d, 1e | 1c, 1d, 1e | 1b, 1c |
| 1.07 | The teacher conducts an ensemble or class using a recorded (MIDI sequenced) accompaniment. | X | X | X | | | | - | 1, 3 | 1d, 1e | 1c, 1d, 1e | 1b, 1c |
| 1.08 | The teacher creates practice recordings for students and burns them to CD. | | X | | | X | | - | 1, 2, 3 | 1d, 1e | 1c, 1d, 1e | 1b, 1c |
| 1.09 | The teacher creates practice recordings (or MIDI sequences) and posts them on the school or music web site. | | X | | | X | | - | 1, 2, 3 | 1d, 1e | 1c, 1d, 1e | 1b, 1c |

Technology Strategies for Music Education:  Appendix A

# TI:ME Technology Strategies

## Organized by MENC Achievement Standards

INST = Electronic Instruments; PROD = Music Production; NOTE = Notation Software,
CAI = Technology-Assisted Learning Software; MULTI = Multimedia; TOOLS = Productivity and Management

### MENC ACHIEVEMENT STANDARD 2

| NUM | STUDENT ACTIVITIES AND TEACHER STRATEGIES | TI:ME AREAS OF TECHNOLOGY | | | | | | ISTE STAND | | MENC ACHV STAND - GRADES | | |
|---|---|---|---|---|---|---|---|---|---|---|---|---|
| | | INST | MUSP ROD | NOTE | CAI | MULTI | TOOLS | NET-S | NETS-T | K-4 | 5-8 | 9-12 |
| 2.01 | The student performs melodic, rhythmic and chordal parts using electronic instruments. | X | | | | | | 1, 3 | - | 2a, 2b, 2c, 2d, 2e, 2f | 2a, 2b, 2c, 2d, 2e | 2a, 2b, 2c |
| 2.02 | The student performs one-on-a-part using electronic instruments. | X | | | | | | 1, 3 | - | 2a, 2b, 2c, 2d, 2e, 2f | 2a, 2b, 2c, 2d, 2e | 2a, 2b, 2c |
| 2.03 | The student learns to play an instrument using appropriate computer-assisted instruction software. | X | | | X | | | 1, 3, 6 | - | 2b | 2b | 2a |
| 2.04 | The student performs music of diverse genres and cultures using electronic keyboard/instruments and sound modules. | X | | | | | | 1, 3 | - | 2c | 2c | 2a |
| 2.05 | The student demonstrates the ability to maintain a steady beat using MIDI percussion controllers or electronic keyboards. | X | | | | | | 1, 3 | - | 2a, 2b, 2d | 2a | 2b |
| 2.06 | The student uses practice and performance devices in rehearsal and/or performance. | X | | | X | | | 1, 3, 6 | - | 1b, 1e | 2c, 2e | 2b, 2c |
| 2.07 | The student searches for MIDI files using the Internet and uses them for practice and performance. | | X | | | | X | 1, 3, 4, 5 | - | 1b, 1e | 2c, 2e' | 2b, 2c |
| 2.08 | The student composes using electronic instruments. | X | | | | | | 1, 3, 6 | - | 2a, 2b, 2d | 2a | 2b |
| 2.09 | The teacher plays accompaniments using music production and/or accompaniment software. | | X | | | | | - | 1, 3 | 1b, 1e | 2c, 2e | 2b,2c |
| 2.10 | The teacher selects appropriate music for students to use in live performance. | X | | | | | | - | 1, 2 | 2e, 2f | 2a, 2c | 2a, 2b, 2c |
| 2.11 | The teacher accesses General MIDI (GM) sounds using a GM instrument or sound module. | X | | | | | | - | 1, 3 | 2a, 2b, 2d | 2a | 2b |
| 2.12 | The teacher uses notation software to compose and print music for electronic instruments. | X | | X | | | | - | 1, 2 | 2a, 2b, 2d | 2a | 2b |

# TI:ME Technology Strategies

## Organized by MENC Achievement Standards

INST = Electronic Instruments; PROD = Music Production; NOTE = Notation Software,
CAI = Technology-Assisted Learning Software; MULTI = Multimedia; TOOLS = Productivity and Management

| MENC ACHIEVEMENT STANDARD 3 | | TI:ME AREAS OF TECHNOLOGY | | | | | | ISTE STAND | | MENC ACHV STAND - GRADES | | |
|---|---|---|---|---|---|---|---|---|---|---|---|---|
| NUM | STUDENT ACTIVITIES AND TEACHER STRATEGIES | INST | MUSP ROD | NOTE | CAI | MULTI | TOOLS | NET-S | NETS-T | K-4 | 5-8 | 9-12 |
| 3.01 | The student improvises melodic phrases and answers using electronic instruments. | X | | | | | | 1, 3 | - | 3a, 3b | 3b | 3a |
| 3.02 | The student improvises simple songs and compositions using a variety of electronic sound sources. | X | | | | | | 1, 3 | - | 3a, 3b, 3c, 3d | 3a, 3b, 3c | 3a, 3b, 3c |
| 3.03 | The student improvises percussion parts using an electronic keyboard. | X | | | | | | 1, 3 | - | 3a, 3b, 3c, 3d | 3a, 3b, 3c | 3a, 3b, 3c |
| 3.04 | The student creates original harmonic progressions using the "single finger" left hand bass function contained on many electronic keyboards. | X | | | | | | 1, 3 | - | - | 3a | 3a |
| 3.05 | The student uses auto-accompaniment software for improvisation. | X | | | X | | | 1, 3 | - | 3a, 3b, 3c, 3d | 3a, 3b, 3c | 3a, 3b, 3c |
| 3.06 | The student records vocal improvisation using music production/digital audio software. | | X | | | | | 1, 3 | - | 3a, 3b, 3c, 3d | 3a, 3b, 3c | 3a, 3b, 3c |
| 3.07 | The student improvises jazz solos. | | X | | | | | 1, 3 | - | 3a, 3b, 3c, 3d | 3a, 3b, 3c | 3a, 3b, 3c |
| 3.08 | The teacher creates ostinatos and accompaniments for student improvisation using music production or intelligent accompanying software. | | X | | | | | - | 1, 2, 3 | 3a, 3b, 3c, 3d | 3a, 3b, 3c | 3a, 3b, 3c |

# TI:ME Technology Strategies

## Organized by MENC Achievement Standards

INST = Electronic Instruments; PROD = Music Production; NOTE = Notation Software,
CAI = Technology-Assisted Learning Software; MULTI = Multimedia; TOOLS = Productivity and Management

### MENC ACHIEVEMENT STANDARD 4

| NUM | STUDENT ACTIVITIES AND TEACHER STRATEGIES | TI:ME AREAS OF TECHNOLOGY | | | | | | ISTE STAND | | MENC ACHV STAND - GRADES | | |
|---|---|---|---|---|---|---|---|---|---|---|---|---|
| | | INST | MUSP ROD | NOTE | CAI | MULTI | TOOLS | NET-S | NETS-T | K-4 | 5-8 | 9-12 |
| 4.01 | The student creates effects to accompany readings and dramatizations using an electronic sound source (MIDI keyboard, MIDI controller). | X | | | | | | 1, 3 | - | 4a | 4c | - |
| 4.02 | The student composes original compositions using software designed for younger students or non-music readers. | | | | X | | | 1, 3 | - | 4a, 4c | 4a, 4c | 4a |
| 4.03 | The student changes the timbres of one or more parts in a prerecorded MIDI sequence. | | X | | | | | 1, | - | 4c | 4c | 4a |
| 4.04 | The student demonstrates the elements of music using music production software. | | X | | | | | 1, 3 | - | 4a, 4b | 4a | 4a |
| 4.05 | The student manipulates audio and MIDI loops to create an original composition. | | X | | | X | | 1, 3 | - | 4c | 4c | 4a |
| 4.06 | The student arranges pieces for various voices or instruments using a notion program. | | | X | | | | 1, 3 | - | 4b | 4a, 4b | 4b, 4c |
| 4.07 | The student composes pieces demonstrating the ranges of traditional instruments using a notation program or music production software. | | | X | | | | 1, 3 | - | - | - | 4c |
| 4.08 | The student records music in step time and real time using music production or music notation program. | | X | X | | | | 1, 3 | - | 4b | 4b | 4b, 4c |
| 4.09 | The student creates compositional forms (ABA, Rondo, theme and variations, and so forth) using a sequencer or notation program. | | X | X | | | | 1, 3 | - | 4b | 4a | 4a |
| 4.10 | The student creates, edits, and stores sounds using a MIDI instrument, a sound source, and editor/librarian software. | X | | | | | | 1, 3 | - | 4c | 4c | 4c |

# TI:ME Technology Strategies

## Organized by MENC Achievement Standards

INST = Electronic Instruments; PROD = Music Production; NOTE = Notation Software,
CAI = Technology-Assisted Learning Software; MULTI = Multimedia; TOOLS = Productivity and Management

| MENC ACHIEVEMENT STANDARD 4 | | TI:ME AREAS OF TECHNOLOGY | | | | | | ISTE STAND | | MENC ACHV STAND - GRADES | | |
| --- | --- | --- | --- | --- | --- | --- | --- | --- | --- | --- | --- | --- |
| NUM | STUDENT ACTIVITIES AND TEACHER STRATEGIES | INST | MUSP ROD | NOTE | CAI | MULTI | TOOLS | NET-S | NETS-T | K-4 | 5-8 | 9-12 |
| 4.11 | The student composes music using algorithmic composition software. | | X | X | | | | 1, 3 | - | - | 4c | 4c |
| 4.12 | The student records a MIDI sequence and synchronizes it with a movie soundtrack, film, or video. | | X | | | X | | 1, 3 | - | - | 4c | 4c |
| 4.13 | The student records and edits acoustic sounds using digital sound editing software. | | X | | | | | 1, 3 | - | - | - | 1a |
| 4.14 | The teacher creates multi-timbral musical examples using music production software. | | X | | | | | - | 1, 2 | 4b | 4a | 4a |
| 4.15 | The teacher creates musically expressive MIDI sequences using appropriate MIDI controllers. | X | X | | | | | - | 1, 2 | 4b | 4a | 4a |
| 4.16 | The teacher edits and performs complex mixing processes, and integrates digital audio with MIDI sequences. | | X | | | | | - | 1, 2 | 4b | 4a | 4a |
| 4.17 | The teacher creates lesson plans for use with music composition by creating files for use with music production and music notation software that students manipulate to create their own compositions. | | X | X | | | X | - | 1, 2, 3 | 4c | 4c | 4a |

# TI:ME Technology Strategies

## Organized by MENC Achievement Standards

INST = Electronic Instruments; PROD = Music Production; NOTE = Notation Software,
CAI = Technology-Assisted Learning Software; MULTI = Multimedia; TOOLS = Productivity and Management

| MENC ACHIEVEMENT STANDARD 5 | | TI:ME AREAS OF TECHNOLOGY | | | | | | ISTE STAND | | MENC ACHV STAND - GRADES | | |
| --- | --- | --- | --- | --- | --- | --- | --- | --- | --- | --- | --- | --- |
| NUM | STUDENT ACTIVITIES AND TEACHER STRATEGIES | INST | MUSP ROD | NOTE | CAI | MULTI | TOOLS | NET-S | NETS-T | K-4 | 5-8 | 9-12 |
| 5.01 | The student notates music on a staff using notation software. | | | X | | | | 1, 3 | - | 5d | 5d | - |
| 5.02 | The student self-evaluates music reading and notation skills using appropriate computer-assisted instruction software. | | | | X | | | 1, 3 | - | 5a, 5b, 5c | 5a, 5b, 5c, 5e | 5a, 5b |
| 5.03 | The student will identify note names and rhythmic values using appropriate CAI software. | | | | X | | | 1, 3 | - | 5a, 5b, 5c | 5a, 5b, 5c, 5e | 5a, 5e |
| 5.04 | The student will solve musical problems requiring the mastery of sound and notation symbols using appropriate CAI software. | | | | X | | | 1, 3 | - | 5a | 5a | 5a |
| 5.05 | The student performs electronic instruments reading printed notation. | X | | X | | | | 1 | - | 5a, 5b, 5c | 5a, 5b, 5c, 5e | 5a, 5b |
| 5.06 | The teacher prints music reading exercises for students using notation software. | | | X | | | | - | 1, 2, 3 | 5a, 5b, 5c, 5d | 5a, 5b, 5c, 5e | 5a, 5b |
| 5.07 | The teacher posts music notation files on the Internet using notation plug-ins for student practice and reference. | | | X | | X | X | - | 1, 2, 3, 4 | 5a, 5b, 5c | 5a, 5b, 5c, 5e | 5a, 5b |
| 5.08 | The teacher saves music notation files in a PDF format for posting on the Internet. | | | X | | X | X | - | 1, 2, 3, 4 | 5a, 5b, 5c | 5a, 5b, 5c, 5e | 5a, 5b |

# TI:ME Technology Strategies

Organized by MENC Achievement Standards

INST = Electronic Instruments; PROD = Music Production; NOTE = Notation Software,
CAI = Technology-Assisted Learning Software; MULTI = Multimedia; TOOLS = Productivity and Management

| MENC ACHIEVEMENT STANDARD 6 | | TI:ME AREAS OF TECHNOLOGY | | | | | | ISTE STAND | | MENC ACHV STAND - GRADES | | |
|---|---|---|---|---|---|---|---|---|---|---|---|---|
| NUM | STUDENT ACTIVITIES AND TEACHER STRATEGIES | INST | MUSP ROD | NOTE | CAI | MULTI | TOOLS | NET-S | NETS-T | K-4 | 5-8 | 9-12 |
| 6.01 | The student develops the ability to recognize and identify specific rhythmic, melodic, and harmonic elements of music using CAI software. | | | | X | | | 1, 3 | - | 6b, 6c | 6a, 6c | 6b |
| 6.02 | The student develops the ability to identify musical forms and recognize similar and contrasting sections using CAI software. | | | | X | X | | 1, 3 | - | 6a | 6a, 6b | 6a |
| 6.03 | The student researches information related to listening such as musical style or historical information using the Internet. | | | | X | | | 1, 3, 4, 5 | - | 6c | 6c | 6c |
| 6.04 | The student writes a review or analysis of music using word processing software. | | | | | | X | 1, 3 | - | - | 6a, 6b, 6c | 6a, 6b, 6c |
| 6.05 | The student demonstrates analytical and listening skills creating a multimedia presentation on a composer or other musical concept. | | | | | X | X | 1, 3, | - | - | - | 6a, 6b, 6c |
| 6.06 | The teacher selects appropriate CAI and multimedia software to help the student build listening and analytical skills. | | | | X | | | - | 1, 2 | 6a, 6b, 6c, 6d | 6a, 6b, 6c | 6a, 6b, 6c |
| 6.07 | The teacher prepares a review or analysis of music for class handouts using word processing software. | | | | | | X | - | 1, 2, 3 | 6a, 6b, 6c, 6d | 6a, 6b, 6c | 6a, 6b, 6c |
| 6.08 | The teacher creates and edits digital media (recordings, videos) for class presentations on listening using appropriate software and hardware. | | | | | X | X | - | 1, 2, 3 | 6a, 6b, 6c, 6d | 6a, 6b, 6c | 6a, 6b, 6c |
| 6.09 | The teacher researches information on music listening using the Internet. | | | | | | X | - | 1, 2 | 6a, 6b, 6c, 6d | 6a, 6b, 6c | 6a, 6b, 6c |
| 6.10 | The teacher presents interactive instruction and listening lessons to the class using the computer to display the information | | | | X | X | X | - | 1, 3 | 6a, 6b, 6c, 6d | 6a, 6b, 6c | 6a, 6b, 6c |

# TI:ME Technology Strategies

## Organized by MENC Achievement Standards

INST = Electronic Instruments; PROD = Music Production; NOTE = Notation Software,
CAI = Technology-Assisted Learning Software; MULTI = Multimedia; TOOLS = Productivity and Management

| MENC ACHIEVEMENT STANDARD 6 | | TI:ME AREAS OF TECHNOLOGY | | | | | | ISTE STAND | | MENC ACHV STAND - GRADES | | |
| --- | --- | --- | --- | --- | --- | --- | --- | --- | --- | --- | --- | --- |
| NUM | STUDENT ACTIVITIES AND TEACHER STRATEGIES | INST | MUSP ROD | NOTE | CAI | MULTI | TOOLS | NET-S | NETS-T | K-4 | 5-8 | 9-12 |
| 6.11 | The teacher prepares custom listening lessons for students using authoring software. | | | | | X | X | - | 1, 2, 3 | 6a, 6b, 6c, 6d | 6a, 6b, 6c | 6a, 6b, 6c |
| 6.12 | The teacher creates examples for students to listen to, analyze and describe using a MIDI sequencer or intelligent accompaniment software. | | X | | | | | - | 1, 2, 3 | 6a, 6b, 6c | 6a, 6b, 6c | 6a, 6b, 6c |
| 6.13 | The teacher prepares a WebQuest for students that provides them with a tool to analyze and describe music of various cultures and genres. | | | | X | | X | - | 1, 2, 3 | 6a, 6b, 6c, 6d | 6a, 6b, 6c | 6a, 6b, 6c |

# TI:ME Technology Strategies

Organized by MENC Achievement Standards

INST = Electronic Instruments; PROD = Music Production; NOTE = Notation Software,
CAI = Technology-Assisted Learning Software; MULTI = Multimedia; TOOLS = Productivity and Management

| MENC ACHIEVEMENT STANDARD 7 | | TI:ME AREAS OF TECHNOLOGY | | | | | | ISTE STAND | | MENC ACHV STAND - GRADES | | |
|---|---|---|---|---|---|---|---|---|---|---|---|---|
| NUM | STUDENT ACTIVITIES AND TEACHER STRATEGIES | INST | MUS PROD | NOTE | CAI | MULTI | TOOLS | NET-S | NETS-T | K-4 | 5-8 | 9-12 |
| 7.01 | The student develops evaluation skills using technology-assisted-learning and multimedia software. | | | | X | X | | 1, 3 | - | 7a, 7b | 7a, 7b | 7a, 7b, 7c |
| 7.02 | The student finds information to aid in the evaluation of music such as background, performance practices, and indicators of quality using the Internet. | | | | | | X | 1, 3, 4, 5 | - | 7a, 7b | 7a, 7b | 7a, 7b, 7c |
| 7.03 | The student uses the Internet to find and download multiple performances of the same work for comparison. | | | | | X | X | 1, 3, 4, 5 | - | 7a, 7b | 7a, 7b | 7a, 7b, 7c |
| 7.04 | The student reads on-line reviews and criticisms of performances and recordings. | | | | X | | X | 1, 3 | - | 7a, 7b | 7a, 7b | 7a, 7b, 7c |
| 7.05 | The student uses the Internet to research the history of music criticism and its impact on composition and performance. | | | | | | X | 1, 3, 4, 5 | - | 7a, 7b | 7a, 7b | 7a, 7b, 7c |
| 7.06 | The student captures musical performances for self-evaluation or evaluation by the teacher using notation or music-production software. | | X | X | | | | 1, 3 | - | - | 7a, 7b | 7b |
| 7.07 | The student designs web pages and multimedia presentations which showcase his or her evaluations of music. | | | | | X | | 1, 3 | - | 7a, 7b | 7a, 7b | 7a, 7b, 7c |
| 7.08 | The student evaluates musical scores and performances on the Internet using a browser with an appropriate plug-in. | | | | | X | X | 1, 4, 5 | - | 7a, 7b | 7a, 7b | 7a, 7b, 7c |
| 7.09 | The teacher selects appropriate technology-assisted lessons and multimedia software to help students build skill in evaluating music. | | | | X | X | | - | 1, 2, 3, 4 | 7a, 7b | 7a, 7b | 7a, 7b, 7c |
| 7.10 | The teacher finds background information, performance practices, and indicators of quality on the evaluation of music using the Internet. | | | | | | X | - | 1, 2, 3, 4 | 7a, 7b | 7a, 7b | 7a, 7b, 7c |

# TI:ME Technology Strategies

### Organized by MENC Achievement Standards

INST = Electronic Instruments; PROD = Music Production; NOTE = Notation Software,
CAI = Technology-Assisted Learning Software; MULTI = Multimedia; TOOLS = Productivity and Management

| MENC ACHIEVEMENT STANDARD 7 | | TI:ME AREAS OF TECHNOLOGY | | | | | | ISTE STAND | | MENC ACHV STAND - GRADES | | |
|---|---|---|---|---|---|---|---|---|---|---|---|---|
| NUM | STUDENT ACTIVITIES AND TEACHER STRATEGIES | INST | MUS PROD | NOTE | CAI | MULTI | TOOLS | NET-S | NETS-T | K-4 | 5-8 | 9-12 |
| 7.11 | The teacher finds multiple performances for students to compare using the Internet. | | | | | | X | - | 1, 2, 3, 4 | 7a, 7b | 7a, 7b | 7a, 7b, 7c |
| 7.12 | The teacher finds on-line review and criticisms of performances and recordings for student use. | | | | | | X | - | 1, 2, 3, 4 | 7a, 7b | 7a, 7b | 7a, 7b, 7c |
| 7.13 | The teacher finds Internet sites which describe the role and history of music criticism. | | | | | | X | - | 1, 2, 3 | 7a, 7b | 7a, 7b | 7a, 7b, 7c |
| 7.14 | The teacher creates examples for students to listen, analyze, and describe using music production or notation software. The examples may be used within the notation software or posted to the Internet for viewing in browsers with an appropriate plug-in. | | | X | | | | - | 1, 2, 3, 4 | 7a, 7b | 7a, 7b | 7a, 7b, 7c |
| 7.15 | The teacher organizes and presents musical excerpts for students to critique using presentation or authoring software. | | | | X | X | | - | 1, 2, 3, 4 | 7a, 7b | 7a, 7b | 7a, 7b, 7c |
| 7.16 | The teacher records and evaluates student performances using intelligent accompaniment software, notation or music-production software. | | X | X | | X | | - | 1, 2, 3, 4 | 7a, 7b | 7a, 7b | 7a, 7b, 7c |
| 7.17 | The teacher prepares scores for the Internet for evaluation by students. | | | X | | X | | - | 1, 2, 3, 4 | 7a, 7b | 7a, 7b | 7a, 7b, 7c |
| 7.18 | The teacher designs web pages and multimedia presentations which help students evaluate music. | | | | | X | | - | 1, 2, 3, 4 | 7a, 7b | 7a, 7b | 7a, 7b, 7c |

# TI:ME Technology Strategies

## Organized by MENC Achievement Standards

INST = Electronic Instruments; PROD = Music Production; NOTE = Notation Software,
CAI = Technology-Assisted Learning Software; MULTI = Multimedia; TOOLS = Productivity and Management

| MENC ACHIEVEMENT STANDARD 8 | | TI:ME AREAS OF TECHNOLOGY | | | | | | ISTE STAND | | MENC ACHV STAND - GRADES | | |
| --- | --- | --- | --- | --- | --- | --- | --- | --- | --- | --- | --- | --- |
| NUM | STUDENT ACTIVITIES AND TEACHER STRATEGIES | INST | MUSP ROD | NOTE | CAI | MULTI | TOOLS | NET-S | NETS-T | K-4 | 5-8 | 9-12 |
| 8.01 | The student learns the relationship between music and the arts and other disciplines using technology-assisted lessons and multimedia software. | | | | X | | | 1, 3 | - | 8a, 8b | 8a, 8b | 8a, 8b, 8c |
| 8.02 | The student compares and contrasts two or more art forms from information gathered from the Internet. | | | | | | X | 1, 3, 4, 5 | - | - | 8a, 8b | 8a, 8b, 8c, 8d, 8e |
| 8.03 | The student creates a multimedia presentation demonstrating the relationship between music and the other arts and disciplines. | | | | | X | X | 1, 3 | - | - | 8a, 8b | 8a, 8b, 8c, 8d, 8e |
| 8.04 | The student uses music production or notation software to create musical accompaniments for other art forms such as ballet, video excerpts, drama, and poetry readings. | | X | X | | | | 1, 3 | - | - | 8a, 8b | 8a, 8b, 8c, 8d, 8e |
| 8.05 | The student uses Internet sites that use music to teach content from other disciplines including songs about the alphabet, math and grammar facts, states and capitals, historic events, the environment, and science concepts. | | | | X | | X | 1, 3, 4, 5 | - | 8a, 8b | 8a, 8b | 8a, 8b, 8c, 8d, 8e |
| 8.06 | The student uses Internet sites which explain concepts from other disciplines which help understand music, its inner workings, its background, and its structure (science, physics, acoustics, engineering, recording, history, language). | | | | X | | X | 1, 3, 4, 5 | - | 8a, 8b | 8a, 8b | 8a, 8b, 8c, 8d, 8e |
| 8.07 | The student completes web quests in which they research issues from the field of music and other disciplines. | | | | X | | X | 1, 3 | - | 8a, 8b | 8a, 8b | 8a, 8b, 8c, 8d, 8e |
| 8.08 | The student designs web pages and multimedia presentations which show the relationship between music, the arts and other disciplines. | | | | | X | | 1, 3 | - | 8a, 8b | 8a, 8b | 8a, 8b, 8c, 8d, 8e |
| 8.09 | The teacher selects appropriate technology-assisted lessons and multimedia software that teach the relationships between music, the arts, and other disciplines. | | | | X | | | - | 1, 2 | 8a, 8b | 8a, 8b | 8a, 8b, 8c, 8d, 8e |

# TI:ME Technology Strategies

## Organized by MENC Achievement Standards

INST = Electronic Instruments; PROD = Music Production; NOTE = Notation Software,
CAI = Technology-Assisted Learning Software; MULTI = Multimedia; TOOLS = Productivity and Management

| | MENC ACHIEVEMENT STANDARD 8 | TI:ME AREAS OF TECHNOLOGY | | | | | | ISTE STAND | | MENC ACHV STAND - GRADES | | |
|---|---|---|---|---|---|---|---|---|---|---|---|---|
| NUM | STUDENT ACTIVITIES AND TEACHER STRATEGIES | INST | MUSP ROD | NOTE | CAI | MULTI | TOOLS | NET-S | NETS-T | K-4 | 5-8 | 9-12 |
| 8.10 | The teacher collects materials which explain the relationships among music, the arts, and other disciplines using the Internet and multimedia reference software. | | | | X | | X | - | 1, 2 | 8a, 8b | 8a, 8b | 8a, 8b, 8c, 8d, 8e |
| 8.11 | The teacher creates web pages and multimedia presentations demonstrating the relationships between music, the arts, and other disciplines. | | | | | X | X | - | 1, 2, 3 | - | 8a, 8b | 8a, 8b, 8c, 8d, 8e |
| 8.12 | The teacher uses music production or notation software to create musical examples to help illustrate connections between music and other art forms such as ballet, video, drama, and poetry. | | X | X | | | | - | 1, 2, 3 | - | 8a, 8b | 8a, 8b, 8c, 8d, 8e |
| 8.13 | The teacher directs the student to Internet sites which use music to help student learn content from other disciplines. | | | | X | | X | - | 1, 2, 3 | 8a, 8b | 8a, 8b | 8a, 8b, 8c, 8d, 8e |
| 8.14 | The teacher directs student to Internet sites which explain the connections between other disciplines and music. | | | | X | | X | - | 1, 2, 3 | 8a, 8b | 8a, 8b | 8a, 8b, 8c, 8d, 8e |
| 8.15 | The teacher designs web quests for students in which they research musical, arts-related, and non-musical topics. | | | | | X | X | - | 1, 2, 3 | 8a, 8b | 8a, 8b | 8a, 8b, 8c, 8d, 8e |

# TI:ME Technology Strategies

Organized by MENC Achievement Standards

INST = Electronic Instruments; PROD = Music Production; NOTE = Notation Software,
CAI = Technology-Assisted Learning Software; MULTI = Multimedia; TOOLS = Productivity and Management

| MENC ACHIEVEMENT STANDARD 9 | | TI:ME AREAS OF TECHNOLOGY | | | | | | ISTE STAND | | MENC ACHV STAND - GRADES | | |
|---|---|---|---|---|---|---|---|---|---|---|---|---|
| NUM | STUDENT ACTIVITIES AND TEACHER STRATEGIES | INST | MUSP ROD | NOTE | CAI | MULTI | TOOLS | NET-S | NETS-T | K-4 | 5-8 | 9-12 |
| 9.01 | The student learns to recognize relationships between music, history, and culture by using technology-assisted lessons. | | | | X | | | 1, 3 | - | - | 9a, 9b, 9c | 9a, 9b, 9d |
| 9.02 | The student creates various tunings on an electronic instrument to demonstrate the evolution of tunings throughout the history of music. | X | | | | | | 1, 3 | - | 9a | 9a | 9a |
| 9.03 | The student locates historical and cultural information using the Internet. | | | | X | | | 1, 3, 4, 5 | - | 9a, 9b, 9d | 9a, 9b, 9c | 9a, 9b, 9c, 9d |
| 9.04 | The student analyzes music of various cultures and musical styles using notation and music-production software. | | X | X | | | | 1, 3 | - | 9a, 9b | 9a, 9b | 9a, 9d |
| 9.05 | The student exchanges information on music, history, and culture with other students throughout the world using Internet services such as chat and e-mail. | | | | | X | X | 1, 3, 4, 5 | - | 9b, 9c, 9d | 9c | 9c, 9d |
| 9.06 | The teacher selects appropriate technology-assisted lessons and multimedia software to teach relationships between music, history, and culture. | | | | X | | | - | 1, 2, 3 | 9a, 9b, 9d | 9a, 9b, 9c | 9a, 9b, 9c, 9d |
| 9.07 | The teacher creates various tunings using an electronic instrument to demonstrate the evolution of tunings throughout the history of music. | X | | | | | | - | 1, 2, 3 | 9a | 9a | 9a |
| 9.08 | The teacher presents the music of various cultures and historical periods using notation and music-production software. | | X | X | | | | - | 1, 2, 3 | 9a, 9b | 9a, 9b | 9a, 9d |
| 9.09 | The teacher finds historical and cultural information for use in class using multimedia programs and the Internet. | | | | X | | X | - | 1, 2, 3, 4, 5 | 9a, 9b, 9d | 9a, 9b, 9c | 9a, 9b, 9c, 9d |
| 9.10 | The teacher collects and shares information about other cultures using the Internet. | | | | | | X | - | 1, 2, 3, 4, 5 | 9b, 9c, 9d | 9c | 9c, 9d |
| 9.11 | The teacher designs web pages and multimedia presentations on the relationship between music, history, and culture. | | | | | X | | - | 1, 2, 3 | 9a, 9b, 9d | 9a, 9b, 9c | 9a, 9b, 9c, 9d |

Technology Strategies for Music Education: Appendix A

# APPENDIX B

## Technology Strategies Organized by TI:ME Technology Areas

The columns in Appendix B are arranged as in Appendix A but they have been organized according to the TI:ME technology areas as described in Section 2. These areas are listed below. Area 6, Productivity Tools, Classroom and Lab Management, is detailed further in Appendix C.

**TI:ME Technology Areas**

1. Electronic Instruments
2. Music Production
3. Notation Software,
4. Technology-Assisted Learning Software
5. Multimedia
6. Productivity Tools, Classroom and Lab Management

# TI:ME Technology Strategies

Organized by TI:ME "Electronic Instrument" Strategy

INST = Electronic Instruments; PROD = Music Production; NOTE = Notation Software,
CAI = Technology-Assisted Learning Software; MULTI = Multimedia; TOOLS = Productivity and Management

## ELECTRONIC INSTRUMENTS

| MENC ACHIEVEMENT STANDARD 1 | | TI:ME AREAS OF TECHNOLOGY | | | | | | ISTE STAND | | MENC ACHV STAND - GRADES | | |
|---|---|---|---|---|---|---|---|---|---|---|---|---|
| NUM | STUDENT ACTIVITIES AND TEACHER STRATEGIES | INST | MUSP ROD | NOTE | CAI | MULTI | TOOLS | NET-S | NETS-T | K-4 | 5-8 | 9-12 |
| 1.06 | The teacher plays accompaniments using music production software. | X | X | | | | | - | 1, 3 | 1d, 1e | 1c, 1d, 1e | 1b, 1c |
| 1.07 | The teacher conducts an ensemble or class using a recorded (MIDI sequenced) accompaniment. | X | X | X | | | | - | 1, 3 | 1d, 1e | 1c, 1d, 1e | 1b, 1c |
| 2.01 | The student performs melodic, rhythmic and chordal parts using electronic instruments. | X | | | | | | 1, 3 | - | 2a, 2b, 2c, 2d, 2e, 2f | 2a, 2b, 2c, 2d, 2e | 2a, 2b, 2c |
| 2.02 | The student performs one-on-a-part using electronic instruments. | X | | | | | | 1, 3 | - | 2a, 2b, 2c, 2d, 2e, 2f | 2a, 2b, 2c, 2d, 2e | 2a, 2b, 2c |
| 2.03 | The student learns to play an instrument using appropriate computer-assisted instruction software. | X | | | X | | | 1, 3, 6 | - | 2b | 2b | 2a |
| 2.04 | The student performs music of diverse genres and cultures using electronic keyboard/instruments and sound modules. | X | | | | | | 1, 3 | - | 2c | 2c | 2a |
| 2.05 | The student demonstrates the ability to maintain a steady beat using MIDI percussion controllers or electronic keyboards. | X | | | | | | 1, 3 | - | 2a, 2b, 2d | 2a | 2b |
| 2.06 | The student uses practice and performance devices in rehearsal and/or performance. | X | | | X | | | 1, 3, 6 | - | 1b, 1e | 2c, 2e | 2b, 2c |
| 2.08 | The student composes using electronic instruments. | X | | | | | | 1, 3, 6 | - | 2a, 2b, 2d | 2a | 2b |
| 2.10 | The teacher selects appropriate music for students to use in live performance. | X | | | | | | - | 1, 2 | 2e, 2f | 2a, 2c | 2a, 2b, 2c |
| 2.11 | The teacher accesses General MIDI (GM) sounds using a GM instrument or sound module. | X | | | | | | - | 1, 3 | 2a, 2b, 2d | 2a | 2b |
| 2.12 | The teacher uses notation software to compose and print music for electronic instruments. | X | | X | | | | - | 1, 2 | 2a, 2b, 2d | 2a | 2b |
| 3.01 | The student improvises melodic phrases and answers using electronic instruments. | X | | | | | | 1, 3 | - | 3a, 3b | 3b | 3a |
| 3.02 | The student improvises simple songs and compositions using a variety of electronic sound sources. | X | | | | | | 1, 3 | - | 3a, 3b, 3c, 3d | 3a, 3b, 3c | 3a, 3b, 3c |

Technology Strategies for Music Education: Appendix B

# TI:ME Technology Strategies

Organized by TI:ME "Electronic Instruments" Strategy

INST = Electronic Instruments; PROD = Music Production; NOTE = Notation Software,
CAI = Technology-Assisted Learning Software; MULTI = Multimedia; TOOLS = Productivity and Management

## ELECTRONIC INSTRUMENTS

| MENC ACHIEVEMENT STANDARD 3 | | TI:ME AREAS OF TECHNOLOGY | | | | | | ISTE STAND | | MENC ACHV STAND - GRADES | | |
|---|---|---|---|---|---|---|---|---|---|---|---|---|
| NUM | STUDENT ACTIVITIES AND TEACHER STRATEGIES | INST | MUSP ROD | NOTE | CAI | MULTI | TOOLS | NET-S | NETS-T | K-4 | 5-8 | 9-12 |
| 3.03 | The student improvises percussion parts using an electronic keyboard. | X | | | | | | 1, 3 | - | 3a, 3b, 3c, 3d | 3a, 3b, 3c | 3a, 3b, 3c |
| 3.04 | The student creates original harmonic progressions using the "single finger" left hand bass function contained on many electronic keyboards. | X | | | | | | 1, 3 | - | - | 3a | 3a |
| 3.05 | The student uses auto-accompaniment software for improvisation. | X | | | X | | | 1, 3 | - | 3a, 3b, 3c, 3d | 3a, 3b, 3c | 3a, 3b, 3c |
| 4.01 | The student creates effects to accompany readings and dramatizations using an electronic sound source (MIDI keyboard, MIDI controller). | X | | | | | | 1, 3 | - | 4a | 4c | - |
| 4.10 | The student creates, edits, and stores sounds using a MIDI instrument, a sound source, and editor/librarian software. | X | | | | | | 1, 3 | - | 4c | 4c | 4c |
| 4.15 | The teacher creates musically expressive MIDI sequences using appropriate MIDI controllers. | X | | | | | | - | 1, 2 | 4b | 4a | 4a |
| 5.05 | The student performs electronic instruments reading printed notation. | X | | X | | | | 1 | - | 5a, 5b, 5c | 5a, 5b, 5c, 5e | 5a, 5b |
| 9.02 | The student creates various tunings on an electronic instrument to demonstrate the evolution of tunings throughout the history of music. | X | | | | | | 1, 3 | - | 9a | 9a | 9a |
| 9.07 | The teacher creates various tunings using an electronic instrument to demonstrate the evolution of tunings throughout the history of music. | X | | | | | | - | 1, 2, 3 | 9a | 9a | 9a |

# TI:ME Technology Strategies

Organized by TI:ME "Music Production" Strategy

INST = Electronic Instruments; PROD = Music Production; NOTE = Notation Software;
CAI = Technology-Assisted Learning Software; MULTI = Multimedia; TOOLS = Productivity and Management

## MUSIC PRODUCTION

| | MENC ACHIEVEMENT STANDARD 1 | TI:ME AREAS OF TECHNOLOGY | | | | | | ISTE STAND | | MENC ACHV STAND - GRADES | | |
|---|---|---|---|---|---|---|---|---|---|---|---|---|
| NUM | STUDENT ACTIVITIES AND TEACHER STRATEGIES | INST | MUSP ROD | NOTE | CAI | MULTI | TOOLS | NET-S | NETS-T | K-4 | 5-8 | 9-12 |
| 1.03 | The student isolates individual parts for singing practice/rehearsal using music production and/or notation software. | | X | X | | | | 1, 3, 6 | - | 1a | 1a, 1b | 1a |
| 1.04 | The student practices singing one on a part using practice and performance devices. | | X | X | X | | | 1, 3, 6 | - | 1a, 1d | 1a, 1b | 1b |
| 1.05 | The student searches for MIDI files using the Internet to use for practice. | | X | X | | | X | 1, 3, 4, 5 | - | 1c | 1c | 1a |
| 1.06 | The teacher plays accompaniments using music production software. | X | X | | | | | - | 1, 3 | 1d, 1e | 1c, 1d, 1e | 1b, 1c |
| 1.07 | The teacher conducts an ensemble or class using a recorded (MIDI sequenced) accompaniment. | X | X | X | | | | - | 1, 3 | 1d, 1e | 1c, 1d, 1e | 1b, 1c |
| 1.08 | The teacher creates practice recordings for students and burns them to CD. | | X | | | X | | - | 1, 2, 3 | 1d, 1e | 1c, 1d, 1e | 1b, 1c |
| 1.09 | The teacher creates practice recordings (or MIDI sequences) and posts them on the school or music web site. | | X | | | X | | - | 1, 2, 3 | 1d, 1e | 1c, 1d, 1e | 1b, 1c |
| 2.07 | The student searches for MIDI files using the Internet and uses them for practice and performance. | | X | | | | X | 1, 3, 4, 5 | - | 1b, 1e | 2c, 2e´ | 2b, 2c |
| 2.09 | The teacher plays accompaniments using music production and/or accompaniment software. | | X | | | | | - | 1, 3 | 1b, 1e | 2c, 2e | 2b,2c |
| 3.06 | The student records vocal improvisation using music production/digital audio software. | | X | | | | | 1, 3 | - | 3a, 3b, 3c, 3d | 3a, 3b, 3c | 3a, 3b, 3c |
| 3.07 | The student improvises jazz solos. | | X | | | | | 1, 3 | - | 3a, 3b, 3c, 3d | 3a, 3b, 3c | 3a, 3b, 3c |
| 3.08 | The teacher creates ostinatos and accompaniments for student improvisation using music production or intelligent accompanying software. | | X | | | | | - | 1, 2, 3 | 3a, 3b, 3c, 3d | 3a, 3b, 3c | 3a, 3b, 3c |

Technology Strategies for Music Education:  Appendix B

# TI:ME Technology Strategies

**Organized by TI:ME "Music Production" Strategy**

INST = Electronic Instruments; PROD = Music Production; NOTE = Notation Software,
CAI = Technology-Assisted Learning Software; MULTI = Multimedia; TOOLS = Productivity and Management

## MUSIC PRODUCTION

| NUM | MENC ACHIEVEMENT STANDARD 4 — STUDENT ACTIVITIES AND TEACHER STRATEGIES | TI:ME AREAS OF TECHNOLOGY | | | | | | ISTE STAND | | MENC ACHV STAND - GRADES | | |
|---|---|---|---|---|---|---|---|---|---|---|---|---|
| | | INST | MUSPROD | NOTE | CAI | MULTI | TOOLS | NET-S | NETS-T | K-4 | 5-8 | 9-12 |
| 4.03 | The student changes the timbres of one or more parts in a prerecorded MIDI sequence. | | X | | | | | 1, | - | 4c | 4c | 4a |
| 4.04 | The student demonstrates the elements of music using music production software. | | X | | | | | 1, 3 | - | 4a, 4b | 4a | 4a |
| 4.05 | The student manipulates audio and MIDI loops to create an original composition. | | X | | | X | | 1, 3 | - | 4c | 4c | 4a |
| 4.08 | The student records music in step time and real time using music production or music notation program. | | X | X | | | | 1, 3 | - | 4b | 4b | 4b, 4c |
| 4.09 | The student creates compositional forms (ABA, Rondo, theme and variations, and so forth) using a sequencer or notation program. | | X | X | | | | 1, 3 | - | 4b | 4a | 4a |
| 4.11 | The student composes music using algorithmic composition software. | | X | X | | | | 1, 3 | - | - | 4c | 4c |
| 4.12 | The student records a MIDI sequence and synchronizes it with a movie soundtrack, film, or video. | | X | | | X | | 1, 3 | - | - | 4c | 4c |
| 4.13 | The student records and edits acoustic sounds using digital sound editing software. | | X | | | | | 1, 3 | - | - | - | 1a |
| 4.14 | The teacher creates multi-timbral musical examples using music production software. | | X | | | | | - | 1, 2 | 4b | 4a | 4a |
| 4.15 | The teacher creates musically expressive MIDI sequences using appropriate MIDI controllers. | X | X | | | | | - | 1, 2 | 4b | 4a | 4a |
| 4.16 | The teacher edits and performs complex mixing processes, and integrates digital audio with MIDI sequences. | | X | | | | | - | 1, 2 | 4b | 4a | 4a |
| 4.17 | The teacher creates lesson plans for student composition by creating files for use with music production and music notation software that students manipulate to create their own compositions. | | X | X | | | X | - | 1, 2, 3 | 4c | 4c | 4a |
| 6.12 | The teacher creates examples for students to listen to, analyze and describe using a MIDI sequencer or intelligent accompaniment software. | | X | | | | | - | 1, 2, 3 | 6a, 6b, 6c | 6a, 6b, 6c | 6a, 6b, 6c |
| 7.06 | The student captures musical performances for self-evaluation or evaluation by the teacher using notation or music-production software. | | X | X | | | | 1, 3 | - | - | 7a, 7b | 7b |
| 7.16 | The teacher records and evaluates student performances using intelligent accompaniment software, notation or music-production software. | | X | X | | X | | - | 1, 2, 3, 4 | 7a, 7b | 7a, 7b | 7a, 7b, 7c |

# TI:ME Technology Strategies

Organized by TI:ME "Music Production" Strategy

INST = Electronic Instruments; PROD = Music Production; NOTE = Notation Software,
CAI = Technology-Assisted Learning Software; MULTI = Multimedia; TOOLS = Productivity and Management

## MUSIC PRODUCTION

| MENC ACHIEVEMENT STANDARD 8 | | TI:ME AREAS OF TECHNOLOGY | | | | | | ISTE STAND | | MENC ACHV STAND - GRADES | | |
|---|---|---|---|---|---|---|---|---|---|---|---|---|
| | | INST | MUSP ROD | NOTE | CAI | MULTI | TOOLS | NET-S | NETS-T | K-4 | 5-8 | 9-12 |
| NUM | STUDENT ACTIVITIES AND TEACHER STRATEGIES | | | | | | | | | | | |
| 8.04 | The student uses music production or notation software to create musical accompaniments for other art forms such as ballet, video excerpts, drama, and poetry readings. | | X | X | | | | 1, 3 | - | - | 8a, 8b | 8a, 8b, 8c, 8d, 8e |
| 8.12 | The teacher uses music production or notation software to create musical examples to help illustrate connections between music and other art forms such as ballet, video, drama, and poetry. | | X | X | | | | - | 1, 2, 3 | - | 8a, 8b | 8a, 8b, 8c, 8d, 8e |
| 9.04 | The student analyzes music of various cultures and musical styles using notation and music-production software. | | X | X | | | | 1, 3 | - | 9a, 9b | 9a, 9b | 9a, 9d |
| 9.08 | The teacher presents the music of various cultures and historical periods using notation and music-production software. | | X | X | | | | - | 1, 2, 3 | 9a, 9b | 9a, 9b | 9a, 9d |

# TI:ME Technology Strategies

## Organized by TI:ME "Notation" Strategy

INST = Electronic Instruments; PROD = Music Production; NOTE = Notation Software,
CAI = Technology-Assisted Learning Software; MULTI = Multimedia; TOOLS = Productivity and Management

## NOTATION

| NUM | STUDENT ACTIVITIES AND TEACHER STRATEGIES | INST | MUSP ROD | NOTE | CAI | MULTI | TOOLS | NET-S | NETS-T | K-4 | 5-8 | 9-12 |
|---|---|---|---|---|---|---|---|---|---|---|---|---|
| | MENC ACHIEVEMENT STANDARD 1 | TI:ME AREAS OF TECHNOLOGY | | | | | | ISTE STAND | | MENC ACHV STAND - GRADES | | |
| 1.03 | The student isolates individual parts for singing practice/rehearsal using music production and/or notation software. | | X | X | | | | 1, 3, 6 | - | 1a | 1a, 1b | 1a |
| 1.04 | The student practices singing one on a part using practice and performance devices. | | X | X | X | | | 1, 3, 6 | - | 1a, 1d | 1a, 1b | 1b |
| 1.05 | The student searches for MIDI files using the Internet to use for practice. | | X | X | | | X | 1, 3, 4, 5 | - | 1c | 1c | 1a |
| 1.07 | The teacher conducts an ensemble or class using a recorded (MIDI sequenced) accompaniment. | X | X | X | | | | - | 1, 3 | 1d, 1e | 1c, 1d, 1e | 1b, 1c |
| 2.12 | The teacher uses notation software to compose and print music for electronic instruments. | X | | X | | | | - | 1, 2 | 2a, 2b, 2d | 2a | 2b |
| 4.06 | The student arranges pieces for various voices or instruments using a notion program. | | | X | | | | 1, 3 | - | 4b | 4a, 4b | 4b, 4c |
| 4.07 | The student composes pieces demonstrating the ranges of traditional instruments using a notation program or music production software. | | | X | | | | 1, 3 | - | - | - | 4c |
| 4.08 | The student records music in step time and real time using music production or music notation program. | | X | X | | | | 1, 3 | - | 4b | 4b | 4b, 4c |
| 4.09 | The student creates compositional forms (ABA, Rondo, theme and variations, and so forth) using a sequencer or notation program. | | X | X | | | | 1, 3 | - | 4b | 4a | 4a |
| 4.11 | The student composes music using algorithmic composition software. | | X | X | | | | 1, 3 | - | - | 4c | 4c |
| 4.17 | The teacher creates lesson plans for student composition by creating files for use with music production and music notation software that students manipulate to create their own compositions. | | X | X | | | X | - | 1, 2, 3 | 4c | 4c | 4a |
| 5.01 | The student notates music on a staff using notation software. | | | X | | | | 1, 3 | - | 5d | 5d | - |
| 5.05 | The student performs electronic instruments reading printed notation. | X | | X | | | | 1 | - | 5a, 5b, 5c | 5a, 5b, 5c, 5e | 5a, 5b |

# TI:ME Technology Strategies

## Organized by TI:ME "Notation" Strategy

INST = Electronic Instruments; PROD = Music Production; NOTE = Notation Software,
CAI = Technology-Assisted Learning Software; MULTI = Multimedia; TOOLS = Productivity and Management

## NOTATION

| MENC ACHIEVEMENT STANDARD 1 | | TI:ME AREAS OF TECHNOLOGY | | | | | | ISTE STAND | | MENC ACHV STAND - GRADES | | |
|---|---|---|---|---|---|---|---|---|---|---|---|---|
| NUM | STUDENT ACTIVITIES AND TEACHER STRATEGIES | INST | MUSP ROD | NOTE | CAI | MULTI | TOOLS | NET-S | NETS-T | K-4 | 5-8 | 9-12 |
| 5.06 | The teacher prints music reading exercises for students using notation software. | | | X | | | | - | 1, 2, 3 | 5a, 5b, 5c, 5d | 5a, 5b, 5c, 5e | 5a, 5b |
| 5.07 | The teacher posts music notation files on the Internet using notation plug-ins for student practice and reference. | | | X | | X | X | - | 1, 2, 3, 4 | 5a, 5b, 5c | 5a, 5b, 5c, 5e | 5a, 5b |
| 5.08 | The teacher saves music notation files in a PDF format for posting on the Internet. | | | X | | X | X | - | 1, 2, 3, 4 | 5a, 5b, 5c | 5a, 5b, 5c, 5e | 5a, 5b |
| 7.06 | The student captures musical performances for self-evaluation or evaluation by the teacher using notation or music-production software. | | X | X | | | | 1, 3 | - | - | 7a, 7b | 7b |
| 7.14 | The teacher creates examples for students to listen, analyze, and describe using music production or notation software. The examples may be used within the notation software or posted to the Internet for viewing in browsers with an appropriate plug-in. | | | X | | | | - | 1, 2, 3, 4 | 7a, 7b | 7a, 7b | 7a, 7b, 7c |
| 7.16 | The teacher records and evaluates student performances using intelligent accompaniment software, notation or music-production software. | | X | X | | X | | - | 1, 2, 3, 4 | 7a, 7b | 7a, 7b | 7a, 7b, 7c |
| 7.17 | The teacher prepares scores for the Internet for evaluation by students. | | | X | | X | | - | 1, 2, 3, 4 | 7a, 7b | 7a, 7b | 7a, 7b, 7c |
| 8.04 | The student uses music production or notation software to create musical accompaniments for other art forms such as ballet, video excerpts, drama, and poetry readings. | | X | X | | | | 1, 3 | - | - | 8a, 8b | 8a, 8b, 8c, 8d, 8e |
| 8.12 | The teacher uses music production or notation software to create musical examples to help illustrate connections between music and other art forms such as ballet, video, drama, and poetry. | | X | X | | | | - | 1, 2, 3 | - | 8a, 8b | 8a, 8b, 8c, 8d, 8e |
| 9.04 | The student analyzes music of various cultures and musical styles using notation and music-production software. | | X | X | | | | 1, 3 | - | 9a, 9b | 9a, 9b | 9a, 9d |
| 9.08 | The teacher presents the music of various cultures and historical periods using notation and music-production software. | | X | X | | | | - | 1, 2, 3 | 9a, 9b | 9a, 9b | 9a, 9d |

# TI:ME Technology Strategies

Organized by TI:ME "Technology-Assisted Learning" Strategy

INST = Electronic Instruments; PROD = Music Production; NOTE = Notation Software,
CAI = Technology-Assisted Learning Software; MULTI = Multimedia; TOOLS = Productivity and Management

## TECHNOLOGY-ASSISTED LEARNING

| MENC ACHIEVEMENT STANDARD 1 | | TI:ME AREAS OF TECHNOLOGY | | | | | | ISTE STAND | | MENC ACHV STAND - GRADES | | |
|---|---|---|---|---|---|---|---|---|---|---|---|---|
| NUM | STUDENT ACTIVITIES AND TEACHER STRATEGIES | INST | MUSP ROD | NOTE | CAI | MULTI | TOOLS | NET-S | NETS-T | K-4 | 5-8 | 9-12 |
| 1.01 | The student improves pitch accuracy using computer-assisted instruction (CAI) software. | | | | X | | | 1, 3, 6 | - | 1a | 1b | 1a |
| 1.02 | The student improves rhythmic accuracy using CAI software. | | | | X | | | 1, 3, 6 | - | 1a | 1b | 1a |
| 1.04 | The student practices singing one on a part using practice and performance devices. | | X | X | X | | | 1, 3, 6 | - | 1a, 1d | 1a, 1b | 1b |
| 2.03 | The student learns to play an instrument using appropriate computer-assisted instruction software. | X | | | X | | | 1, 3, 6 | - | 2b | 2b | 2a |
| 2.06 | The student uses practice and performance devices in rehearsal and/or performance. | X | | | X | | | 1, 3, 6 | - | 1b, 1e | 2c, 2e | 2b, 2c |
| 3.05 | The student uses auto-accompaniment software for improvisation. | X | | | X | | | 1, 3 | - | 3a, 3b, 3c, 3d | 3a, 3b, 3c | 3a, 3b, 3c |
| 4.02 | The student composes original compositions using software designed for younger students or non-music readers. | | | | X | | | 1, 3 | - | 4a, 4c | 4a, 4c | 4a |
| 5.02 | The student self-evaluates music reading and notation skills using appropriate computer-assisted instruction software. | | | | X | | | 1, 3 | - | 5a, 5b, 5c | 5a, 5b, 5c, 5e | 5a, 5b |
| 5.03 | The student will identify note names and rhythmic values using appropriate CAI software. | | | | X | | | 1, 3 | - | 5a, 5b, 5c | 5a, 5b, 5c, 5e | 5a, 5e |
| 5.04 | The student will solve musical problems requiring the mastery of sound and notation symbols using appropriate CAI software. | | | | X | | | 1, 3 | - | 5a | 5a | 5a |
| 6.01 | The student develops the ability to recognize and identify specific rhythmic, melodic, and harmonic elements of music using CAI software. | | | | X | | | 1, 3 | - | 6b, 6c | 6a, 6c | 6b |
| 6.02 | The student develops the ability to identify musical forms and recognize similar and contrasting sections using CAI software. | | | | X | X | | 1, 3 | - | 6a | 6a, 6b | 6a |
| 6.03 | The student researches information related to listening such as musical style or historical information using the Internet. | | | | X | | X | 1, 3, 4, 5 | - | 6c | 6c | 6c |

# TI:ME Technology Strategies

Organized by TI:ME "Technology-Assisted Learning" Strategy

INST = Electronic Instruments; PROD = Music Production; NOTE = Notation Software,
CAI = Technology-Assisted Learning Software; MULTI = Multimedia; TOOLS = Productivity and Management

## TECHNOLOGY-ASSISTED LEARNING

### MENC ACHIEVEMENT STANDARD 1

| NUM | STUDENT ACTIVITIES AND TEACHER STRATEGIES | TI:ME AREAS OF TECHNOLOGY | | | | | | ISTE STAND | | MENC ACHV STAND - GRADES | | |
|---|---|---|---|---|---|---|---|---|---|---|---|---|
| | | INST | MUSP ROD | NOTE | CAI | MULTI | TOOLS | NET-S | NETS-T | K-4 | 5-8 | 9-12 |
| 6.06 | The teacher selects appropriate CAI and multimedia software to help the student build listening and analytical skills. | | | | X | | | - | 1, 2 | 6a, 6b, 6c, 6d | 6a, 6b, 6c | 6a, 6b, 6c |
| 6.10 | The teacher presents interactive instruction and listening lessons to the class using the computer to display the information | | | | X | X | X | - | 1, 3 | 6a, 6b, 6c, 6d | 6a, 6b, 6c | 6a, 6b, 6c |
| 6.13 | The teacher prepares a Web Quest for students that provides them with a tool to analyze and describe music of various cultures and genres. | | | | X | X | X | - | 1, 2, 3 | 6a, 6b, 6c, 6d | 6a, 6b, 6c | 6a, 6b, 6c |
| 7.01 | The student develops evaluation skills using technology-assisted-learning and multimedia software. | | | | X | X | | 1, 3 | - | 7a, 7b | 7a, 7b | 7a, 7b, 7c |
| 7.04 | The student reads on-line reviews and criticisms of performances and recordings. | | | | X | | X | 1, 3 | - | 7a, 7b | 7a, 7b | 7a, 7b, 7c |
| 7.09 | The teacher selects appropriate technology-assisted lessons and multimedia software to help students build skill in evaluating music. | | | | X | X | | - | 1, 2, 3, 4 | 7a, 7b | 7a, 7b | 7a, 7b, 7c |
| 7.15 | The teacher organizes and presents musical excerpts for students to critique using presentation or authoring software. | | | | X | X | | - | 1, 2, 3, 4 | 7a, 7b | 7a, 7b | 7a, 7b, 7c |
| 8.01 | The student learns the relationship between music and the arts and other disciplines using technology-assisted lessons and multimedia software. | | | | X | | | 1, 3 | - | 8a, 8b | 8a, 8b | 8a, 8b, 8c |
| 8.05 | The student uses Internet sites that use music to teach content from other disciplines including songs about the alphabet, math and grammar facts, states and capitals, historic events, the environment, and science concepts. | | | | X | | X | 1, 3, 4, 5 | - | 8a, 8b | 8a, 8b | 8a, 8b, 8c, 8d, 8e |
| 8.06 | The student uses Internet sites which explain concepts from other disciplines which help understand music, its inner workings, its background, and its structure (science, physics, acoustics, engineering, recording, history, language). | | | | X | | X | 1, 3, 4, 5 | - | 8a, 8b | 8a, 8b | 8a, 8b, 8c, 8d, 8e |
| 8.07 | The student completes web quests in which they research issues from the field of music and other disciplines. | | | | X | | X | 1, 3 | - | 8a, 8b | 8a, 8b | 8a, 8b, 8c, 8d, 8e |
| 8.09 | The teacher selects appropriate technology-assisted lessons and multimedia software that teach the relationships between music, the arts, and other disciplines. | | | | X | | | - | 1, 2 | 8a, 8b | 8a, 8b | 8a, 8b, 8c, 8d, 8e |
| 8.10 | The teacher collects materials which explain the relationships among music, the arts, and other disciplines using the Internet and multimedia reference software. | | | | X | | X | - | 1, 2 | 8a, 8b | 8a, 8b | 8a, 8b, 8c, 8d, 8e |

Technology Strategies for Music Education:  Appendix B

# TI:ME Technology Strategies

Organized by TI:ME "Technology-Assisted Learning" Strategy

INST = Electronic Instruments; PROD = Music Production; NOTE = Notation Software,
CAI = Technology-Assisted Learning Software; MULTI = Multimedia; TOOLS = Productivity and Management

## TECHNOLOGY-ASSISTED LEARNING

| MENC ACHIEVEMENT STANDARD 1 | | TI:ME AREAS OF TECHNOLOGY | | | | | | ISTE STAND | | MENC ACHV STAND - GRADES | | |
|---|---|---|---|---|---|---|---|---|---|---|---|---|
| NUM | STUDENT ACTIVITIES AND TEACHER STRATEGIES | INST | MUSP ROD | NOTE | CAI | MULTI | TOOLS | NET-S | NETS-T | K-4 | 5-8 | 9-12 |
| 8.13 | The teacher directs the student to Internet sites which use music to help student learn content from other disciplines. | | | | X | | X | - | 1, 2, 3 | 8a, 8b | 8a, 8b | 8a, 8b, 8c, 8d, 8e |
| 8.14 | The teacher directs student to Internet sites which explain the connections between other disciplines and music. | | | | X | | X | - | 1, 2, 3 | 8a, 8b | 8a, 8b | 8a, 8b, 8c, 8d, 8e |
| 9.01 | The student learns to recognize relationships between music, history, and culture by using technology-assisted lessons. | | | | X | | | 1, 3 | - | - | 9a, 9b, 9c | 9a, 9b, 9d |
| 9.03 | The student locates historical and cultural information using the Internet. | | | | X | | X | 1, 3, 4, 5 | - | 9a, 9b, 9d | 9a, 9b, 9c | 9a, 9b, 9c, 9d |
| 9.06 | The teacher selects appropriate technology-assisted lessons and multimedia software to teach relationships between music, history, and culture. | | | | X | | | - | 1, 2, 3 | 9a, 9b, 9d | 9a, 9b, 9c | 9a, 9b, 9c, 9d |
| 9.09 | The teacher finds historical and cultural information for use in class using multimedia programs and the Internet. | | | | X | | X | - | 1, 2, 3, 4, 5 | 9a, 9b, 9d | 9a, 9b, 9c | 9a, 9b, 9c, 9d |

# TI:ME Technology Strategies

## Organized by TI:ME "Multimedia" Strategy

INST = Electronic Instruments; PROD = Music Production; NOTE = Notation Software,
CAI = Technology-Assisted Learning Software; MULTI = Multimedia; TOOLS = Productivity and Management

## MULTIMEDIA

| NUM | STUDENT ACTIVITIES AND TEACHER STRATEGIES | INST | MUSP ROD | NOTE | CAI | MULTI | TOOLS | NET-S | NETS-T | K-4 | 5-8 | 9-12 |
|---|---|---|---|---|---|---|---|---|---|---|---|---|
| | **MENC ACHIEVEMENT STANDARD 1** | **TI:ME AREAS OF TECHNOLOGY** | | | | | | **ISTE STAND** | | **MENC ACHV STAND - GRADES** | | |
| 1.08 | The teacher creates practice recordings for students and burns them to CD. | | X | | | X | | - | 1, 2, 3 | 1d, 1e | 1c, 1d, 1e | 1b, 1c |
| 1.09 | The teacher creates practice recordings (or MIDI sequences) and posts them on the school or music web site. | | X | | | X | | - | 1, 2, 3 | 1d, 1e | 1c, 1d, 1e | 1b, 1c |
| 4.05 | The student manipulates audio and MIDI loops to create an original composition. | | X | | | X | | 1, 3 | - | 4c | 4c | 4a |
| 4.12 | The student records a MIDI sequence and synchronizes it with a movie soundtrack, film, or video. | | X | | | X | | 1, 3 | - | - | 4c | 4c |
| 5.07 | The teacher posts music notation files on the Internet using notation plug-ins for student practice and reference. | | | X | | X | X | - | 1, 2, 3, 4 | 5a, 5b, 5c | 5a, 5b, 5c, 5e | 5a, 5b |
| 5.08 | The teacher saves music notation files in a PDF format for posting on the Internet. | | | X | | X | X | - | 1, 2, 3, 4 | 5a, 5b, 5c | 5a, 5b, 5c, 5e | 5a, 5b |
| 6.02 | The student develops the ability to identify musical forms and recognize similar and contrasting sections using CAI software. | | | | X | X | | 1, 3 | - | 6a | 6a, 6b | 6a |
| 6.05 | The student demonstrates analytical and listening skills creating a multimedia presentation on a composer or other musical concept. | | | | | X | X | 1, 3, | - | - | - | 6a, 6b, 6c |
| 6.08 | The teacher creates and edits digital media (recordings, videos) for class presentations on listening using appropriate software and hardware. | | | | | X | X | - | 1, 2, 3 | 6a, 6b, 6c, 6d | 6a, 6b, 6c | 6a, 6b, 6c |
| 6.10 | The teacher presents interactive instruction and listening lessons to the class using the computer to display the information | | | | X | X | X | - | 1, 3 | 6a, 6b, 6c, 6d | 6a, 6b, 6c | 6a, 6b, 6c |
| 6.11 | The teacher prepares custom listening lessons for students using authoring software. | | | | | X | X | - | 1, 2, 3 | 6a, 6b, 6c, 6d | 6a, 6b, 6c | 6a, 6b, 6c |

Technology Strategies for Music Education: Appendix B

# TI:ME Technology Strategies

Organized by TI:ME "Multimedia" Strategy

INST = Electronic Instruments; PROD = Music Production; NOTE = Notation Software,
CAI = Technology-Assisted Learning Software; MULTI = Multimedia; TOOLS = Productivity and Management

## MULTIMEDIA

| NUM | STUDENT ACTIVITIES AND TEACHER STRATEGIES | TI:ME AREAS OF TECHNOLOGY | | | | | | ISTE STAND | | MENC ACHV STAND - GRADES | | |
|---|---|---|---|---|---|---|---|---|---|---|---|---|
| | | INST | MUS PROD | NOTE | CAI | MULTI | TOOLS | NET-S | NETS-T | K-4 | 5-8 | 9-12 |
| 7.01 | The student develops evaluation skills using technology-assisted-learning and multimedia software. | | | | X | X | | 1, 3 | - | 7a, 7b | 7a, 7b | 7a, 7b, 7c |
| 7.03 | The student uses the Internet to find and download multiple performances of the same work for comparison. | | | | | X | X | 1, 3, 4, 5 | - | 7a, 7b | 7a, 7b | 7a, 7b, 7c |
| 7.07 | The student designs web pages and multimedia presentations which showcase his or her evaluations of music. | | | | | X | | 1, 3 | - | 7a, 7b | 7a, 7b | 7a, 7b, 7c |
| 7.08 | The student evaluates musical scores and performances on the Internet using a browser with an appropriate plug-in. | | | | | X | X | 1, 4, 5 | - | 7a, 7b | 7a, 7b | 7a, 7b, 7c |
| 7.09 | The teacher selects appropriate technology-assisted lessons and multimedia software to help students build skill in evaluating music. | | | | X | X | | - | 1, 2, 3, 4 | 7a, 7b | 7a, 7b | 7a, 7b, 7c |
| 7.15 | The teacher organizes and presents musical excerpts for students to critique using presentation or authoring software. | | | | X | X | | - | 1, 2, 3, 4 | 7a, 7b | 7a, 7b | 7a, 7b, 7c |
| 7.16 | The teacher records and evaluates student performances using intelligent accompaniment software, notation or music-production software. | | X | | | X | | - | 1, 2, 3, 4 | 7a, 7b | 7a, 7b | 7a, 7b, 7c |
| 7.17 | The teacher prepares scores for the Internet for evaluation by students. | | | X | | X | | - | 1, 2, 3, 4 | 7a, 7b | 7a, 7b | 7a, 7b, 7c |
| 7.18 | The teacher designs web pages and multimedia presentations, which help students, evaluate music. | | | | | X | | - | 1, 2, 3, 4 | 7a, 7b | 7a, 7b | 7a, 7b, 7c |
| 8.03 | The student creates a multimedia presentation demonstrating the relationship between music and the other arts and disciplines. | | | | | X | X | 1, 3 | - | - | 8a, 8b | 8a, 8b, 8c, 8d, 8e |
| 8.08 | The student designs web pages and multimedia presentations which show the relationship between music, the arts and other disciplines. | | | | | X | | 1, 3 | - | 8a, 8b | 8a, 8b | 8a, 8b, 8c, 8d, 8e |
| 8.11 | The teacher creates web pages and multimedia presentations demonstrating the relationships between music, the arts, and other disciplines. | | | | | X | X | - | 1, 2, 3 | - | 8a, 8b | 8a, 8b, 8c, 8d, 8e |
| 8.15 | The teacher designs web quests for students in which they research musical, arts-related, and non-musical topics. | | | | | X | X | - | 1, 2, 3 | 8a, 8b | 8a, 8b | 8a, 8b, 8c, 8d, 8e |
| 9.05 | The student exchanges information on music, history, and culture with other students throughout the world using Internet services such as chat and e-mail. | | | | | X | X | 1, 3, 4, 5 | - | 9b, 9c, 9d | 9c | 9c, 9d |
| 9.11 | The teacher designs web pages and multimedia presentations on the relationship between music, history, and culture. | | | | | X | | - | 1, 2, 3 | 9a, 9b, 9d | 9a, 9b, 9c | 9a, 9b, 9c, 9d |

# TI:ME Technology Strategies

Organized by TI:ME "Productivity and Management" Strategy

INST = Electronic Instruments; PROD = Music Production; NOTE = Notation Software,
CAI = Technology-Assisted Learning Software; MULTI = Multimedia; TOOLS = Productivity and Management

## PRODUCTIVITY AND MANAGEMENT

| NUM | STUDENT ACTIVITIES AND TEACHER STRATEGIES | INST | MUSPROD | NOTE | CAI | MULTI | TOOLS | NET-S | NETS-T | K-4 | 5-8 | 9-12 |
|---|---|---|---|---|---|---|---|---|---|---|---|---|
| 1.05 | The student searches for MIDI files using the Internet to use for practice. | | X | X | | | X | 1, 3, 4, 5 | - | 1c | 1c | 1a |
| 2.07 | The student searches for MIDI files using the Internet and uses them for practice and performance. | | X | X | | | X | 1, 3, 4, 5 | - | 1b, 1e | 2c, 2e' | 2b, 2c |
| 4.17 | The teacher creates lesson plans for student composition by creating files for use with music production and music notation software that students manipulate to create their own compositions. | | X | X | | | X | - | 1, 2, 3 | 4c | 4c | 4a |
| 5.07 | The teacher posts music notation files on the Internet using notation plug-ins for student practice and reference. | | | X | | X | X | - | 1, 2, 3, 4 | 5a, 5b, 5c | 5a, 5b, 5c, 5e | 5a, 5b |
| 5.08 | The teacher saves music notation files in a PDF format for posting on the Internet. | | | X | | X | X | - | 1, 2, 3, 4 | 5a, 5b, 5c | 5a, 5b, 5c, 5e | 5a, 5b |
| 6.03 | The student researches information related to listening such as musical style or historical information using the Internet. | | | | X | | X | 1, 3, 4, 5 | - | 6c | 6c | 6c |
| 6.04 | The student writes a review or analysis of music using word processing software. | | | | | | X | 1, 3 | - | - | 6a, 6b, 6c | 6a, 6b, 6c |
| 6.05 | The student demonstrates analytical and listening skills creating a multimedia presentation on a composer or other musical concept. | | | | | X | X | 1, 3, | - | - | - | 6a, 6b, 6c |
| 6.07 | The teacher prepares a review or analysis of music for class handouts using word processing software. | | | | | | X | - | 1, 2, 3 | 6a, 6b, 6c, 6d | 6a, 6b, 6c | 6a, 6b, 6c |
| 6.08 | The teacher creates and edits digital media (recordings, videos) for class presentations on listening using appropriate software and hardware. | | | | | X | X | - | 1, 2, 3 | 6a, 6b, 6c, 6d | 6a, 6b, 6c | 6a, 6b, 6c |
| 6.09 | The teacher researches information on music listening using the Internet. | | | | | | X | - | 1, 2 | 6a, 6b, 6c, 6d | 6a, 6b, 6c | 6a, 6b, 6c |
| 6.10 | The teacher presents interactive instruction and listening lessons to the class using the computer to display the information | | | | X | X | X | - | 1, 3 | 6a, 6b, 6c, 6d | 6a, 6b, 6c | 6a, 6b, 6c |
| 6.11 | The teacher prepares custom listening lessons for students using authoring software. | | | | | X | X | - | 1, 2, 3 | 6a, 6b, 6c, 6d | 6a, 6b, 6c | 6a, 6b, 6c |
| 6.13 | The teacher prepares a Web Quest for students that provides them with a tool to analyze and describe music of various cultures and genres. | | | | X | | X | - | 1, 2, 3 | 6a, 6b, 6c, 6d | 6a, 6b, 6c | 6a, 6b, 6c |

# TI:ME Technology Strategies

Organized by TI:ME "Productivity and Management" Strategy

INST = Electronic Instruments; PROD = Music Production; NOTE = Notation Software,

CAI = Technology-Assisted Learning Software; MULTI = Multimedia; TOOLS = Productivity and Management

## PRODUCTIVITY AND MANAGEMENT

| NUM | STUDENT ACTIVITIES AND TEACHER STRATEGIES | TI:ME AREAS OF TECHNOLOGY | | | | | | ISTE STAND | | MENC ACHV STAND - GRADES | | |
|---|---|---|---|---|---|---|---|---|---|---|---|---|
| | | INST | MUS PROD | NOTE | CAI | MULTI | TOOLS | NET-S | NETS-T | K-4 | 5-8 | 9-12 |
| 7.02 | The student finds information to aid in the evaluation of music such as background, performance practices, and indicators of quality using the Internet. | | | | | | X | 1, 3, 4, 5 | - | 7a, 7b | 7a, 7b | 7a, 7b, 7c |
| 7.03 | The student uses the Internet to find and download multiple performances of the same work for comparison. | | | | | X | X | 1, 3, 4, 5 | - | 7a, 7b | 7a, 7b | 7a, 7b, 7c |
| 7.04 | The student reads on-line reviews and criticisms of performances and recordings. | | | | X | | X | 1, 3 | - | 7a, 7b | 7a, 7b | 7a, 7b, 7c |
| 7.05 | The student uses the Internet to research the history of music criticism and its impact on composition and performance. | | | | | | X | 1, 3, 4, 5 | - | 7a, 7b | 7a, 7b | 7a, 7b, 7c |
| 7.08 | The student evaluates musical scores and performances on the Internet using a browser with an appropriate plug-in. | | | | | X | X | 1, 4, 5 | - | 7a, 7b | 7a, 7b | 7a, 7b, 7c |
| 7.10 | The teacher finds background information, performance practices, and indicators of quality on the evaluation of music using the Internet. | | | | | | X | - | 1, 2, 3, 4 | 7a, 7b | 7a, 7b | 7a, 7b, 7c |
| 7.11 | The teacher finds multiple performances for students to compare using the Internet. | | | | | | X | - | 1, 2, 3, 4 | 7a, 7b | 7a, 7b | 7a, 7b, 7c |
| 7.12 | The teacher finds on-line review and criticisms of performances and recordings for student use. | | | | | | X | - | 1, 2, 3, 4 | 7a, 7b | 7a, 7b | 7a, 7b, 7c |
| 7.13 | The teacher finds Internet sites which describe the role and history of music criticism. | | | | | | X | - | 1, 2, 3 | 7a, 7b | 7a, 7b | 7a, 7b, 7c |
| 8.02 | The student compares and contrasts two or more art forms from information gathered from the Internet. | | | | | | X | 1, 3, 4, 5 | - | - | 8a, 8b | 8a, 8b, 8c, 8d, 8e |
| 8.03 | The student creates a multimedia presentation demonstrating the relationship between music and the other arts and disciplines. | | | | | X | X | 1, 3 | - | - | 8a, 8b | 8a, 8b, 8c, 8d, 8e |
| 8.05 | The student uses Internet sites that use music to teach content from other disciplines including songs about the alphabet, math and grammar facts, states and capitals, historic events, the environment, and science concepts. | | | | X | | X | 1, 3, 4, 5 | - | 8a, 8b | 8a, 8b | 8a, 8b, 8c, 8d, 8e |
| 8.06 | The student uses Internet sites which explain concepts from other disciplines which help understand music, its inner workings, its background, and its structure (science, physics, acoustics, engineering, recording, history, language). | | | | X | | X | 1, 3, 4, 5 | - | 8a, 8b | 8a, 8b | 8a, 8b, 8c, 8d, 8e |
| 8.07 | The student completes web quests in which they research issues from the field of music and other disciplines. | | | | X | | X | 1, 3 | - | 8a, 8b | 8a, 8b | 8a, 8b, 8c, 8d, 8e |
| 8.10 | The teacher collects materials which explain the relationships among music, the arts, and other disciplines using the Internet and multimedia reference software. | | | | X | | X | - | 1, 2 | 8a, 8b | 8a, 8b | 8a, 8b, 8c, 8d, 8e |

# TI:ME Technology Strategies

Organized by TI:ME "Productivity and Management" Strategy

INST = Electronic Instruments; PROD = Music Production; NOTE = Notation Software,
CAI = Technology-Assisted Learning Software; MULTI = Multimedia; TOOLS = Productivity and Management

## PRODUCTIVITY AND MANAGEMENT

| MENC ACHIEVEMENT STANDARD 7 | | TI:ME AREAS OF TECHNOLOGY | | | | | | ISTE STAND | | MENC ACHV STAND - GRADES | | |
|---|---|---|---|---|---|---|---|---|---|---|---|---|
| NUM | STUDENT ACTIVITIES AND TEACHER STRATEGIES | INST | MUS PROD | NOTE | CAI | MULTI | TOOLS | NET-S | NETS-T | K-4 | 5-8 | 9-12 |
| 8.11 | The teacher creates web pages and multimedia presentations demonstrating the relationships between music, the arts, and other disciplines. | | | | | X | X | - | 1, 2, 3 | - | 8a, 8b | 8a, 8b, 8c, 8d, 8e |
| 8.13 | The teacher directs the student to Internet sites which use music to help student learn content from other disciplines. | | | | X | | X | - | 1, 2, 3 | 8a, 8b | 8a, 8b | 8a, 8b, 8c, 8d, 8e |
| 8.14 | The teacher directs student to Internet sites which explain the connections between other disciplines and music. | | | | X | | X | - | 1, 2, 3 | 8a, 8b | 8a, 8b | 8a, 8b, 8c, 8d, 8e |
| 8.15 | The teacher designs web quests for students in which they research musical, arts-related, and non-musical topics. | | | | | X | X | - | 1, 2, 3 | 8a, 8b | 8a, 8b | 8a, 8b, 8c, 8d, 8e |
| 9.03 | The student locates historical and cultural information using the Internet. | | | | X | | X | 1, 3, 4, 5 | - | 9a, 9b, 9d | 9a, 9b, 9c | 9a, 9b, 9c, 9d |
| 9.05 | The student exchanges information on music, history, and culture with other students throughout the world using Internet services such as chat and e-mail. | | | | | X | X | 1, 3, 4, 5 | - | 9b, 9c, 9d | 9c | 9c, 9d |
| 9.09 | The teacher finds historical and cultural information for use in class using multimedia programs and the Internet. | | | | X | | X | - | 1, 2, 3, 4, 5 | 9a, 9b, 9d | 9a, 9b, 9c | 9a, 9b, 9c, 9d |
| 9.10 | The teacher collects and shares information about other cultures using the Internet. | | | | | | X | - | 1, 2, 3, 4, 5 | 9b, 9c, 9d | 9c | 9c, 9d |

# APPENDIX C

**Technology Strategies Related to Information Processing,
Computer Systems, and Lab Management.**

The tables in Appendix C include the following information:

| TIME NUM | Strategies | IP | CS | LM |
|---|---|---|---|---|
| TI:ME's Technology Area 6 includes three sub-parts:  Information Processing (IP), Computer Systems (CS), and Lab Management (LM).  For example information processing includes 10 strategies, numbers IP01 through IP10.1 | See Section 6. | | | |

# TI:ME Technology Strategies

IP = Information Processing, CS = Computer Systems, LM = Lab Management

| TIME NUM | TEACHER STRATEGIES | IP | CS | LM |
|---|---|---|---|---|
| IP 01 | The teacher creates letters to parents, memos to colleagues, and handouts for students using word processing software. | X | | |
| IP 02 | The teacher averages grades, tracks fundraising projects, and prepares budgets using spreadsheet software. | X | | |
| IP 03 | The teacher organizes class lists, keeps records on uniform and instrument inventory, and maintains a music library using database software. | X | | |
| IP 04 | The teacher creates newsletters and other documents using desktop publishing software. | X | | |
| IP 05 | The teacher creates programs, concert announcements, and banners using general and special -purpose graphics programs. | X | | |
| IP 06 | The teacher uses specialty or specific purpose software (worksheet creation, calendar making, and grade averaging) as needed. | X | | |
| IP 07 | The teacher creates "overhead" materials for class using presentation software. | X | | |
| IP 08 | The teacher creates custom technology-assisted lessons for students using authoring software. | X | | |
| IP 09 | The teacher creates drill charts using marching band show design software. | X | | |
| IP 10 | The teacher uses Internet services such as browsing, electronic mail, instant messaging, list servers, and chat rooms for music learning. | X | | |

| TIME NUM | TEACHER STRATEGIES | IP | CS | LM |
|---|---|---|---|---|
| CS 01 | The teacher uses peripheral audio devices in a music technology lab. | | X | |
| CS 02 | The teacher lists and identifies the components of a computer system and can prepare a proposal for the purchase or upgrade of equipment. | | X | |
| CS 03 | The teacher connects and installs components of a computer system. | | X | |
| CS 04 | The teacher installs and connects peripheral equipment to a computer system. | | X | |
| CS 05 | The teacher installs, operates, and troubleshoots computer operating systems (Windows, Mac OS). | | X | |
| CS 06 | The teacher installs software which limits user access to specific programs and data, thereby protecting the computer hard drive and system software. | | X | |
| CS 07 | The teacher installs and operates a virus protection software. | | X | |
| CS 08 | The teacher connects a single computer to the Internet. | | X | |
| CS 09 | The teacher is aware of copyright restrictions as applied to computer software and other files. | | X | |
| CS 10 | The teacher can describe issues related to connecting electronic instruments for-performance. | | X | |
| CS 11 | The teacher sets up and uses electronic instruments. | | X | |
| CS 12 | The teacher sets up and uses multiple electronic instruments in performance. | | X | |

| TIME NUM | TEACHER STRATEGIES | IP | CS | LM |
|---|---|---|---|---|
| LM 01 | The teacher designs the physical set-up of a computer lab and/or electronic instruments. | | | X |
| LM 02 | The teacher uses appropriate software and hardware to connect computers to form a network. | | | X |
| LM 03 | The teacher connects a computer lab to the Internet. | | | X |
| LM 04 | The teacher uses appropriate software and hardware in a lab of electronic instruments to allow individual and group practice; to listen to and monitor student progress; and to lecture and perform to the entire class, individuals or small groups. | | | X |
| LM 05 | The teacher develops and maintains a budget for the purchase and updating of a computer/technology lab. | | | X |
| LM 06 | The teacher designs lessons for use in a music technology lab. | | | X |

Technology Strategies for Music Education:  Appendix C

# APPENDIX D

**Strategies and Standards at a Glance**

# TI:ME Technology Strategies

1. Electronic Instruments
2. Music Production
3. Notation Software,
4. Technology-Assisted Learning Software
5. Multimedia
6. Productivity and Management

# ISTE
# National Educational Technology Standards

NETS-S
1. Basic operations and concepts
2. Social, ethical, and human issues
3. Technology productivity tools
4. Technology communications tools
5. Technology research tools
6. Technology problem-solving and decision-making tools

NETS-T
1. Technology operations and concepts
2. Planning and Designing Learning Environments and Experiences
3. Teaching, Learning, and the Curriculum
4. Assessment and Evaluation
5. Productivity and Professional Practice
6. Social, Ethical, Legal, and Human Issues

# MENC Curriculum Standards

1. Sing, alone and with others, a varied repertoire of music.
2. Perform on instruments, alone and with others, a varied repertoire of music.
3. Improvise melodies, variations, and accompaniments.
4. Compose and arrange music within specified guidelines.
5. Read and notate music.
6. Listen to, analyze, and describe music.
7. Evaluate music and music performances.
8. Understand relationships among music, the other arts, and disciplines outside the arts.
9. Understand music in relation to history and culture.

# APPENDIX E

## Web Resources

### TECHNOLOGY STRATEGIES WEB RESOURCES
### ISTE/NETS RESOURCES

| *ISTE/NETS WEB RESOURCES* | |
|---|---|
| **Program** | **URL** |
| ISTE Web Site | cnets.iste.org/ |
| NETS-S Foundation Standards and a link to their Performance Indicators | cnets.iste.org/students/s_stands.html |
| NETS-T Foundation Standards and a link to the Performance Indicators | cnets.iste.org/teachers/t_stands.html |
| Additional information about NETS-A | cnets.iste.org/administrators/a_stands.html |
| Bauer, W. I. (2002). Technology standards for music teacher education. | atmi2002.billbauer.net |

This site is maintained by Dr. Kim Walls, Auburn University.
http://www.ti-me.org/technologystrategies/iste/
If a link above does not work, please notify timemused@ti-me.org.
Include the location and the title of this page.
Thank you!

# TECHNOLOGY STRATEGIES WEB RESOURCES
## ASSESSMENT RESOURCES

| *Creating Rubrics.* | |
|---|---|
| **Web Site** | **URL** |
| *RubiStar* | rubistar.4teachers.org/ |
| Rubric Builder | www.landmark-project.com/classweb/tools/rubric_builder.php3 |

| *Electronic Portfolios* | |
|---|---|
| **Web Site** | **URL** |
| electronicportfolios.org | www.electronicportfolios.org/ |

| *Selected Quiz Programs* | | |
|---|---|---|
| **Program** | **URL** | |
| Hot Potatoes | www.halfbakedsoftware.com/ | Macintosh/Wintel |
| QuizMaker Pro | www.classonesoftware.com/C_htmls/QuizMaker.html | Macintosh/Wintel |
| StarFacts | cosmicsoft.net/starFacts/ | Macintosh |
| StarQuiz | cosmicsoft.net/starQuiz/ | Macintosh/Wintel |
| What Do You Know? | www.classonesoftware.com/C_htmls/WDYK.html | Macintosh/Wintel |

| *Selected Grade Book Programs* | | |
|---|---|---|
| **Program** | **URL** | |
| Easy Grade Pro | www.orbissoft.com/ | Macintosh/Wintel |
| Excel * | www.microsoft.com/excel | Macintosh/Wintel |
| GradeKeeper | www.gradekeeper.com/ | Macintosh/Wintel |
| Master Grade | www.maxium.com/ | Macintosh/Wintel |
| MicroGrade | www.chariot.com/micrograde/ | Macintosh/Wintel |

* Excel is not a dedicated grade book program, however it can be used to create a grade book.  Excel-based grade book templates are also available on the Microsoft web site and from other sources.

This site is maintained by Dr. William Bauer, Case Western Reserve University.
http://www.ti-me.org/technologystrategies/assessment/
If a link above does not work, please notify timemused@ti-me.org.
Include the location and the title of this page.
Thank you!